Elder abuse in perspective

RETHINKING AGEING SERIES

Series editor: Brian Gearing
                School of Health and Social Welfare
                The Open University

The rapid growth in ageing populations in Britain and other countries has led to a dramatic increase in academic and professional interest in the subject. Over the past decade this has led to the publication of many research studies which have stimulated new ideas and fresh approaches to understanding old age. At the same time, there has been concern about continued neglect of ageing and old age in the education and professional training of most workers in health and social services, and about inadequate dissemination of the new information and ideas about ageing to a wider public.

This series aims to fill a gap in the market for accessible, up-to-date studies of important issues in ageing. Each book will focus on a topic of current concern addressing two fundamental questions: what is known about this topic? And what are the policy, service and practice implications of our knowledge? Authors will be encouraged to develop their own ideas, drawing on case material, and their own research, professional or personal experience. The books will be interdisciplinary, and written in clear, non-technical language which will appeal to a broad range of students, academics and professionals with a common interest in ageing and age care.

Current and forthcoming titles:
Simon Biggs, Chris Phillipson and Paul Kingston: **Elder abuse in perspective**
Ken Blakemore and Margaret Boneham: **Age, race and ethnicity: A comparative approach**
Joanna Bornat (ed.): **Reminiscence reviewed: Perspectives, evaluations, achievements**
Joanna Bornat and Maureen Cooper: **Older learners**
Bill Bytheway: **Ageism**
Beverley Hughes: **Older people and community care: Critical theory and practice**
Anne Jamieson: **Comparing policies of care for older people**
Sheila Peace *et al.*: **Re-evaluating residential care**
Moyra Sidell: **Health in old age: Myth, mystery and management**
Andrew Sixsmith: **Quality of life: Rethinking well-being in old age**
Robert Slater: **The psychology of growing old: Looking forward**

Elder abuse in perspective

SIMON BIGGS,
CHRIS PHILLIPSON
and
PAUL KINGSTON

OPEN UNIVERSITY PRESS
Buckingham · Philadelphia

Open University Press
Celtic Court
22 Ballmoor
Buckingham
MK18 1XW

and
1900 Frost Road, Suite 101
Bristol, PA 19007, USA

First Published 1995

A catalogue record of this book is available from the British Library

ISBN 0 335 19146 0 (pb)   0 335 19147 9 (hb)

Library of Congress Cataloging-in-Publication Data

Biggs, Simon, 1955–
    Elder abuse in perspective/Simon Biggs, Chris Phillipson, and Paul Kingston.
        p.   cm. — (Rethinking ageing series)
    Includes bibliographical references and index.
    ISBN 0–335–19146–0 (pb) ISBN 0–335–19147–9 (hb)
    1. Aged — Abuse of.   2. Aged — Government policy.   3. Aged — Services for.
    I. Phillipson, Chris.   II. Kingston, Paul.   III. Title.   IV. Series.
    HV6626.3.B53   1995
    362.7 — dc20   95–15366
                                                                       CIP

Typeset by Type Study, Scarborough
Printed in Great Britain by Biddles Limited, Guildford and Kings Lynn

Contents

Series editor's preface

The main aim of the 'Rethinking Ageing' series is to fill the gap between what we now know about older people and ageing populations as a consequence of the considerable expansion of gerontological research in the last two decades, and the relatively limited amount of that knowledge and information which is accessible and readily available to professional and voluntary workers, and others involved with older people. The series has so far focused on major topics of current concern or interest to that audience – race and ethnicity, reminiscence, health and illness, and ageism (to be followed shortly by books on the psychology of growing old, and community care practice). However, these books have also proved attractive to another audience – lecturers, researchers and post-graduate students – which indicates that they are also fulfilling a need amongst academics for a concise and critical overview of what is currently known about important contemporary topics in gerontology.

Elder abuse in perspective fits well into this framework. The abuse and neglect of older people should undoubtedly be an issue of major concern. But it is also an issue which has been characterized by a lack of conceptual and definitional clarity – about what exactly elder abuse is, and what policies and other measures should be adopted in response to it. This book offers a reconceptualization of the topic and is therefore very appropriate for a series whose rationale is to *rethink* contemporary topics in ageing. It will be of equal interest to practitioners, researchers and professional trainers in the health and social services.

Abuse of older people has been slow to receive full recognition as a major issue in gerontology. In a review of the first British book on the topic, Mervyn Eastman's *Old Age Abuse* (1984), Jim Traynor (1985) asked the pertinent question 'Why have British researchers left this area alone?'. Ten years later a raised level of awareness of the problem is still much needed. Elder abuse remains under-recognized and insufficiently acknowledged. This contrasts with child abuse and domestic violence which, as Biggs *et al.* observe, came to prominence during the 1970s through the efforts of grass-roots action and professional concern. Even the excellent textbook in social gerontology, *Ageing in Society: an introduction to social gerontology*, which was published in a second edition less than two years ago (Bond *et al.* 1993), only contains two brief references to abuse, reflecting the paucity of research and critical thought on this topic.

Elder Abuse in Perspective should help to change this situation. Although there have been several other publications on old-age abuse in recent years, this book can claim to be the most critical, comprehensive, and substantive exploration of the subject to be published in the United Kingdom so far. It provides a much needed coherent view of what elder abuse is, why it occurs, and how practitioners and others might respond. The authors describe the aims of their book succinctly '[it] has a dual purpose: first, to map out an area which is beginning to be identified as significant in both the research and social policy arenas; second, to say something about the difficulties associated with talking about abuse and neglect: How do we define the problem? How is its existence best explained? What are the different reasons for abuse – in institutional in contrast to family settings? On what basis could effective interventions be made?'.

As this suggests, its explanatory breadth exceeds that of books which have sought only to describe the phenomenon of elder abuse and to discuss its implications for practice. This is not a manual, or a 'cookbook', which simply gives recipes for good practice in cases of suspected elder abuse. The authors are clear that a theoretical perspective is important because explicit or implicit theories of abuse causation always underpin decisions about intervention and influence its nature. Those who make such decisions need a coherent framework for considering the key issues involved in intervention. Responsible and reflective practice must be guided by theoretical awareness. In addressing the question – 'Why does elder abuse happen?' – Biggs *et al.* do not simply accept explanations imported from studies of child abuse and domestic violence. Rather, their explanatory framework is grounded in their analysis of the social position of older adults in the UK and other Western societies. This study begins therefore to provide the kind of theoretical understanding which until now has been lacking in the practice of social gerontology.

A brief look at the chapter headings will indicate the broad perspective and comprehensive coverage the authors adopt. Thus, whilst Chapter 1 (Historical perspectives), Chapter 2 (Theoretical issues) and Chapter 3 (Definitions and risk factors) are broadly concerned with explaining and defining abuse; Chapter 5 (Family and community) and Chapter 6 (Institutional care and elder mistreatment) are about the locations where abuse occurs; and Chapter 4 (Social policy), Chapter 7 (Training and elder abuse) and Chapter 8 (Interventions) are about actual and recommended responses to elder abuse and neglect. Throughout the book, the topic is situated in the context of research, policy and practice in various Western countries (e.g. Australia, the USA and elsewhere in Europe), although the most detailed focus is on the UK. The final chapter places the issue of abuse and neglect within the context of gerontological theory, and in doing so makes some specific proposals for tackling the conditions which give rise to abuse and neglect.

One reason advanced by Biggs *et al.* for the difficulty in achieving the serious recognition of elder abuse as an urgent social problem (in contrast with other kinds of abuse), has been the low status of professionals and carers working with older people. Perhaps for similar reasons, the professional and academic literature on this subject has (with a very few important exceptions) lagged behind that on child abuse in the UK. This book should contribute much to ensuring that elder abuse is finally accorded the importance it merits both in gerontology and as an area of social and professional concern.

Brian Gearing
School of Health and Social Welfare
The Open University

References

Bond, J., Coleman, P. and Peace, S. (1993) *Ageing in Society: an introduction to social gerontology.* London: Sage.

Eastman, M. (1984) *Old Age Abuse.* Mitcham, Surrey: Age Concern England.

Traynor, J. (1985) Review of Mervyn Eastman's *Old Age Abuse. Ageing and Society,* 5(1): 141–2.

Acknowledgements

The idea for this book was first raised by Brian Gearing and the authors owe him a considerable debt of gratitude for his encouragement during the preparation of the manuscript. The book has also benefited from complementary research and debate that has emerged amongst British researchers over the past five years. We would especially like to mention the work of Gerry Bennett and Frank Glendenning, both of whom have made distinctive contributions to the reassessment of the field of elder abuse.

The team at Open University Press have been highly supportive, and we are particularly grateful to Jacinta Evans, Joan Malherbe and Claire Hutchins.

At Keele itself, colleagues in the Department of Applied Social Studies, and the Gerontology group in particular, have provided a lively sounding board for ideas. The book has greatly benefited from secretarial help at different stages, and Michelle Briggs deserves particular mention for her hard work on the book.

Finally, we must also mention our partners – Angela, Clare and Jane – who have given considerable support during the book's preparation. Their help has been vital to the task of getting our own thoughts in order and bringing the project to completion.

Introduction

The abuse and neglect of older people has been the subject of study and debate in the United States for approximately 15 years. In UK settings and the rest of Europe, Canada and Australia, it has only recently been identified as an emerging social problem that requires a definite response at the levels of policy, agency activity and professional behaviour.

The goal for work in this field should be to ensure that older people can enjoy a life free of violence and mistreatment. The route to achieving this goal is complex and difficult. It would involve the development of social policy that recognizes, rather than colludes with, ageist assumptions that form a backdrop to abuse and neglect. Similarly, it would require that services are developed that both recognize the special needs of our fellow citizens who live to an old age, and are sensitively attuned to the issues surrounding instances of maltreatment.

This book has two main purposes. First, as an increasing number of instances of abuse and neglect are coming to the attention of health, welfare and criminal justice services, helping professionals need to understand the nature of the problem and some of the actions that can be taken to alleviate it. Second, the time has come to stand back from what can be a disturbing and emotionally charged subject area, and place the phenomenon within its historical, sociological and psychological context. It is not, then, our intention to have written a text that is primarily promotional in the approach it takes. Neither is it a cookbook of the 'this is what you must do' variety. Rather, it is hoped that the reader will be encouraged to engage in reflective study and practice, and will obtain a deeper insight into the way that elder maltreatment has been constructed as a social problem and develop a considered perspective from which to intervene.

Use of terms

It is difficult in a relatively new and changing field to find agreement on a generic term to describe the phenomenon under study. As Chapter 3 shows, a number of terms have been used to describe the abuse and neglect of older people, by different authors and at different times throughout the evolution of understanding of the subject itself. There are two questions to address here. First, what is the best way to refer to people over the age of 65? Second, how should abusive and neglectful activities be described?

On the first of these questions there seems to be general agreement amongst students of older age, or gerontologists, of a need to use a term that is both descriptive and which either gives a neutral or positive connotation to those at the top of the life course (Bytheway 1994). We have followed this understanding by using 'older people' and 'elders' to describe such individuals or groups. 'Older people' conveys the fact that we see our chosen subjects as people, that is, citizens with the same human and civil rights as the rest of the adult population. It also conveys their special status in life course terms, the older group of citizens who may also have particular requirements. 'Elders' is used more or less interchangeably with 'older people', and its use is intended to emphasize the positive aspects that old age can confer. Whilst terms such as 'elderly', for example as in the 'elderly population', may occasionally be used, we consider that this term is best avoided if it reinforces the view of older people as a homogeneous bloc of the population. This is both depersonalizing as well as inaccurate as a description of older people at the turn of the century.

When it comes to the second question, we have tended to use 'abuse and neglect' and the term 'mistreatment' to refer to the negative conditions that certain older people have to endure. If 'abuse' is used on its own, then the reader should assume that we mean that, rather than a shorthand for the above. This reflects our intention that the book be primarily about active abuse rather than passive neglect. 'Mistreatment' emphasizes the negative and destructive nature of such situations or actions, which, as the argument that we pursue will suggest, are often of a complex and confusing nature if one is seeking a clear victim and perpetrator. Occasionally the reader may find reference to 'maltreatment', as a means of making the text readable and not too repetitive. The multiple use of terms to some extent reflects the developing nature of research and practice in this area, as illustrated in Chapters 1 and 2.

With regard to other terms used, 'carer' and occasionally 'informal carer' have been used to describe people, usually, but not exclusively, relatives, who are looking after another person. These must be distinguished from 'paid carers', who are also referred to as 'professional helpers' or 'workers' or by their particular vocational label.

Overview of contents

Chapter 1: Historical perspectives

The book begins by placing the current growth in awareness of elder mistreatment within a historical context. Whilst abuse and neglect have been with us across the centuries, public concern has waxed and waned. In some historical periods, for example during the witchcraft crazes of the sixteenth and seventeenth centuries, violence and murder of older women received official sanction. The chapter shows that the emergence of abuse as a social problem has been closely tied to changes in the economic basis of Western society. At different times, the relationship between community, family and institutional care and the recognition of what was thought of as abusive within such contexts has varied. The particular problems that we now associate with older age only really became an issue at the end of the nineteenth century, where they were seen from the perspective of destitution and neglect. We have arguably had to wait until the 1970s for questions to be asked about the sanctity of specifically family settings. This was a period when child abuse and domestic violence came to prominence through the efforts of grass roots action and professional concern (Kingston and Penhale 1995). Elder abuse is a late addition to this roll call of damage to people's lives and, as will be returned to throughout the book, is still in the process of achieving full recognition.

Chapter 2: Theoretical issues

This chapter provides the reader with a guide to the main theoretical arguments that have been used to explain elder mistreatment. A distinction is made between pragmatic approaches and conceptual approaches. Explanations are thought to be pragmatic if they have arisen from existing responses to similar social problems. They are, in other words, drawn from related fields of practice, such as child protection and domestic violence. The advantages and disadvantages of using these frameworks for understanding the abuse and neglect of older people are discussed. By conceptual approaches we mean theories that have been used to explain broader social and psychological phenomena, of which elder abuse is a specific example. Research evidence is reviewed to give readers some idea of the value of the different perspectives that have resulted. We conclude by proposing that to understand the phenomenon at least three levels of analysis are required: first, the way in which elder abuse and neglect has been socially and historically constructed; second, the interplay between key figures within that context; third, the way that the problem is conceived, psychologically, by the individuals involved. The chapter also examines the concept of citizenship as a means of bringing together some of the issues involved in the categorization of individuals as abused or maltreated.

Chapter 3: Definitions and risk factors

Definitions and theories are important because they shape what we look for and how we respond to social problems. Risk factors give us some idea of the likelihood that some form of abuse or neglect is taking place. Whilst most people can recognize instances of abuse and neglect when they are shown to them, such phenomena have proved very difficult to define adequately. Reasons for this have included the different professional backgrounds of practitioners, competing theoretical positions adopted by researchers, and the motivations of pressure groups and policy advisers. The chapter outlines a number of definitions and examines the range of research that has under-pinned them. There prove to be very few pieces of research with a sufficiently robust research design for valid conclusions to be drawn. Those studies that meet such criteria are then used to suggest risk factors that can aid helping professionals in the task of identifying potentially abusive situations. These themes are picked up again in Chapters 5 and 6.

Chapter 4: Social policy

In this chapter we consider the pathway that elder abuse and neglect have taken in becoming a social problem, in other words, how 'social problem status' has been achieved. It picks up where historical perspectives left off in considering contemporary policy responses. Social policy, in this sense, goes beyond simply describing any official government response; rather, the chapter examines how these responses actually shape and position the problem in comparison with other policy issues. The chapter is divided into sections which describe developments in Australia, Europe and North America, and draws lessons for future policy and practice. A section has been reserved for the consideration of UK social policy and its relationship to political priorities of the day. British social policy would seem to have a tradition which, whilst self-neglect has been considered, has devoted little space to the need for elder protection. It is argued that locating abuse within the family serves certain political objectives which have resulted in other contexts being eclipsed from view.

Chapter 5: Family and community

The argument begun in the preceding chapter is continued here by examining the relationship between family, community and responses to mistreatment in some depth. We begin by noting that notions of family, and specifically care for older people in families, are subject to competing and emotionally charged value systems. Concerns about responsibilities and benefits, obligation and choice, place practitioners on a delicate tightrope which divides private and public space. Somehow the private world of the family and the public expectations that professionals represent and are charged with enforcing have to be negotiated without losing sight of the possibility of abuse. Government guidance on elder protection is critically analysed and compared with research evidence in a number of key areas. Notions of carer stress, role reversal and an obligation to care, which may seem to be common sense at first glance, are shown to be largely unsupported. The opportunities and pitfalls represented by contemporary practice in the community are also reviewed, including care management and the tricky questions of reporting and visibility. Some areas are found to be in need of greater attention, most notably the community harassment of older people, financial abuse and the capacity of relatives to care.

Chapter 6: Institutional care and elder mistreatment

Whilst current thinking has largely focused on the family as the site of abuse and neglect, this chapter serves as a grim reminder of an enduring history of institutional abuse of older people. Questions are raised concerning whether institutions should be thought of as abusive in themselves, or whether under some circumstances they can improve an elder's quality of life. Subsequent sections outline indicators that can be used to assess the likelihood of abuse and neglect in residential and long-stay settings, the role of workplace morale on care quality and steps that can be taken to put things right. It seems that in many cases it would be mistaken to blame individual workers exclusively if acts of abuse and neglect are discovered. These are usually symptoms of a deeper malaise concerning the culture of the institution at issue, the failure of management systems and deteriorated relations with the outside world.

Chapter 7: Training and elder abuse

Elder abuse is a relatively recent concern for helping agencies, and brings with it a need for adequate training. This chapter establishes certain principles thought to be necessary if training is to be made successful. Training initiatives are examined as events in themselves and as a contribution to wider organizational change. Programme planning is broken down into a number of stages: preparation, the training intervention itself, and consolidation once the formal input has been concluded. However, it is argued that discrete training initiatives can be successful only as part of a wider project to influence the culture of an organization. Examples are given which emphasize the importance of multidisciplinary collaboration, plus the coordination of training with policy and procedural developments.

Chapter 8: Interventions

This chapter reviews and assesses a number of methods that have been used in the UK and in North America to intervene in cases of elder mistreatment. Such an appraisal has to take into account the move from a position where abuse was contained within dense kinship structures and large-scale institutions, to one where it takes place within more fragmented family structures and relatively small-scale residential settings. Community development, advocacy and mediation are currently under-used in UK settings and hold considerable promise as a means of negotiating change. Models based on the prevention of domestic violence, social work intervention and legal intervention are considered in turn. Whilst it is argued that US experience highlights the dangers of criminalization, a sensitive and discriminating use of care management, refuges, victim support and anger management groups should be encouraged. Different methods of intervention will be most appropriate at different times, depending on the nature of abuse taking place and its severity. A picture emerges of a variety of preventive and protective measures that could be made available if elder mistreatment were to be seen as a resource priority.

Conclusions

In a concluding chapter the book places the issue of abuse and neglect within the wider framework of gerontological theory. A number of proposals emerge from this in terms of taking the debate forward, both in the arena of broad social policy and in respect of work within families and special settings.

Elder mistreatment is emerging as a growing social problem in most Western societies. We hope that readers will find this book to be a helpful guide both in terms of the current state of knowledge on the subject and in promoting reflective and effective practice.

1

Historical perspectives

Introduction

In the mid-1970s, a new phrase entered the lexicon of the caring professions – that of 'granny battering' (Baker 1975; Burston 1977). In Britain, doctors and social workers began, from this period, to document cases of people subject to often severe instances of cruelty and neglect. Mervyn Eastman (1983, 1984), who was to become a leading figure in the debate, produced a monograph detailing numerous cases from his own records and from other contacts with older people as well as informal carers (Eastman 1984a). Few could doubt, from the nature of his descriptions, that an important area of concern had been identified. Yet, shocking as the cases he identified certainly were, it might be argued that they made little immediate impact, either on the community of professionals concerned with caring for older people or on the wider society. The reasons for this were probably threefold.

First, the professions involved with older people were still having to adjust to the various other forms of family violence identified in the 1960s and 1970s (notably child abuse and violence to women). Set in this context, the problems of 'battered grannies' struggled to gain serious acknowledgement. Added to this was the low status of professionals concerned with caring for older people, these often being the least well qualified and worst paid in their respective groups (Phillipson 1982; Biggs 1993a). Such factors limited the extent to which the issue of abuse would be taken seriously or treated with any degree of urgency. An additional reason, however, was the status of older people in post-war British society. Fennell et al. (1988: 6) have described the 'welfarization' of elderly people in this period, this involving they suggest, a subtle mixture of diminution and patronage. The authors write:

> There may be nothing wrong with welfare, as such, but there is a risk that
> the people we welfarize, we do not allow fully human stature: they are not

quite whole people, not people like us. They are only one step removed from the 'poor dears' in nursing homes whom other elderly people are said to patronize in the subtle stratification system of the disadvantaged.

The idea of the 'abused elder' seemed to fit, therefore, an existing stereotype which emphasized the marginality of the old. Indeed, it was difficult to separate cause and effect: were older people marginalized because of experiences such as abuse? Alternatively, did elder abuse emerge from the numerous medical and social problems which seemed to comprise the lives of the majority of older people?

A final factor which hindered the debate on abuse was the term itself. Very few commentaries in this field can resist expressing concern at the range of definitions of abuse and/or their lack of precision (Johnson 1991; Pitt 1992; see also Chapter 3). However, it would be more surprising if there were clarity and agreement in this area given the nature of the subject matter. We are dealing, after all, with covert and overt conflict in social relationships, private (in domestic settings), semi-public (in the special settings of residential homes and related forums), and public (in the wider society). Framing the nature of this conflict into precise concepts is fraught with difficulty: there will always be a degree of selectivity in whom we decide is being abused, and in what we see as representative of abuse. Moreover, as Glendenning (1993) remarks, definitions of the problem will tend to vary according to who is expressing concern: the victim, the carer, the physician, the nurse, the social worker, and so on. None of this is to say that the concept is worthless or to trivialize the experiences of those older people affected. It is, however, to suggest a degree of caution in terms of how we interpret issues in the debate about abuse and to recognize the difficulties of both analysis and intervention.

The purpose of this chapter is to explore a range of issues concerned with the placing of abuse and maltreatment of older people in a historical context. The chapter will consider the variety of tensions – social and familial – which have characterized the lives of older people. It will review some of the major influences on kinship relations and the impact of these on the treatment of the elderly. The chapter will argue that we have entered a distinctive period in the history of abuse and neglect, one which reflects significant changes in both the position of older people, and their experience of dependency within a range of social institutions.

Historical issues in the development of abuse

Social tensions of different kinds have been ever-present in the lives of elderly people. The possibility of intergenerational conflict has arisen through: the elders' control over property and the resulting frustrations of younger kin (Thomas 1976; Stearns 1986); the pressures faced by an unmarried daughter left to care for her parents (Bardwell 1926); or the crisis generated through economic recession, as families have struggled with the contradictions of meeting the care needs of both older and younger generations (Murphy 1931).

More generally, Minois (1989) in his *History of Old Age*, examining the period from antiquity to the Renaissance, suggests that ambivalence has been a recurring theme in social attitudes towards older people, with the stress laid upon physical strength and bodily vigour creating problems for groups such as older people.

The treatment of elders is also bound up with the history of the poor and the varied experiences of those without an independent income. From the seventeenth century onwards, attitudes have moved backwards and forwards, from the scapegoating of the destitute in periods of economic hardship, to the provision of almshouses and other forms of charitable giving. More generally, older people have struggled to stay in their own homes or have lived with their children, albeit with frequent reminders of the limits to their authority (Anderson 1974; Thomas 1976; Stone 1978; Laudrie 1980).

Overall, the consensus from historians is that tensions between the old and the young (or, to be completely accurate, the middle aged) were a persistent feature of family relations in the pre-modern era. Peter Stearns (1986: 6) observes:

> In some European countries, the elderly were carefully housed separately from younger kin, once the latter had acquired property control. Small cottages built to the rear of the main dwelling may have reduced daily disputes but they may also have symbolized the lack of mutual interests that could produce tension. Many older people were forced into almshouses and hospitals, both of which were, well into the 19th century, dominated by the elderly, even though they were not expressly designed for them. To be sure many of these impoverished old people had no families available at all; some had never married; some had families that were simply too poor to offer relief. But some families tried to cast dependent elderly out, even against community norms that tried to maintain responsibility in such cases.

Keith Thomas (1976: 273) notes a 'hostility towards those who opted out of the economic process and reluctance to devote much of society's resources to their maintenance'. He comments also that outside their own families, the relief of the elderly poor was often a low priority and in the village could be bitterly resented (see also Anderson 1974). Even (or especially) within the family, there were pressures. The incomes of poor families could be stretched to breaking point with events such as the birth of a child or loss of employment. Olwen Hufton (1967: 84), writing about the residents of eighteenth-century Bayeux in France, comments: 'The seamstresses, laundresses, and servants of the town . . . worked long hours for a pittance which could only maintain them as long as they were childless or did not have to maintain an aged relative'.

The theme of the 'burden' of the old is reflected in the witchcraft craze that swept through many parts of Western society during the sixteenth and seventeenth centuries (Thomas 1971). Groups such as elderly women were especially vulnerable to accusations of witchcraft, and the incidence of such allegations almost certainly increased during periods of economic distress. Keith Thomas (1971: 672) argues that:

> Population pressure eroded many of the old customary tenancies, and led to the taking in of the commons and the rise in competitive rents. These

changes were disadvantageous to the widow. So were the enclosures and engrossing which broke up many of the old cooperative village communities. This deterioration in the position of the dependent and elderly helps to explain why witches were predominantly women, and probably old ones, many of them widowed. 'They are usually such as are destitute of friends, bowed down with years, laden with infirmities', said a contemporary. Their names appear among the witchcraft indictments, just as they do among the recipients of parochial relief. For they were the persons most dependent upon neighbourly support.

Such allegations may perhaps be seen as an early form of abuse, representing as they do a form of scapegoating for what were natural disasters. More precisely, witchcraft accusations focused upon fears about the consequences of failing to support those who need help in the community. On the one side, a person's reputation for witchcraft might be crucial in ensuring she received relief within the village. On the other, such allegations could be used to justify refusal to give assistance to groups such as the old and infirm. Thomas (1971: 676) notes:

> These two different ways of treating a witch were not really inconsistent, for it was only the person suspected of witchcraft who was to be turned away; and such a suspicion was unlikely to arise so long as men were neighbourly and charitable. Witch-beliefs, in other words, upheld the conventions of charity and neighbourliness, but once these conventions had broken down they justified the breach and made it possible for the uncharitable to divert attention from their own guilt by focusing attention to that of the witch.

Less dramatic, and almost certainly more common, were the everyday pressures affecting older people with limited or non-existent resources. Begging – an early sign of elderly neglect – was commonplace amongst the old, although the elderly were often seen as a 'deserving' case. Hufton (1974), in her study of the poor in eighteenth-century France, records the 'privilege' of the old to beg respectably. Hufton observes (1967: 112):

> They might, with dignity, beg in the churches, and they had a kind of monopoly of the privilege to sit in the porch or on the steps of churches and to make their requests. In parishes in the Auvergne, where begging had been reduced to a fine art, the aged beggar was the only one who caught the eye, for he or she alone remained to beg all the year round, whereas the adult males and most of the children had left on their seasonal odysseys.

It would be wrong to surmise from all this that older people were invariably locked in conflict within the family. Peter Stearns (1986) is right to conclude that not all older men and women were deprived of respect. And there are certainly regional and cultural variations in the status of the old which challenge simple generalizations (Fischer 1989). Moreover, to set against the theme of the 'abandonment of the old', there was the regularization of support through, in the case of Britain, the 1601 Poor Law. From this point, parishes became responsible for supporting groups such as the old and infirm living within their boundaries. David Thomson (1984) has argued that provision through the Poor Law was in many respects remarkably generous. From the seventeenth until the nineteenth century, parish records indicate that over one-half of widows would normally have been provided with regular pensions on the rates, with the level of these being generous in comparison with state pensions in the twentieth century.

Poor Law provision would, then, have played an important role in relieving tensions within the family. On the other hand, a combination of social and economic changes were to threaten the level of support available. These changes almost certainly introduced new problems and difficulties into the lives of older people. It is to a discussion of these that we now turn.

Social policy and the elderly

By the nineteenth century there was a new set of pressures facing older people. Issues relating to the support of elderly people were highlighted by the 1834 Poor Law Amendment Act, this emphasizing the importance of the family in helping the old. In fact, for a period at least, attempts to enforce the legal obligations raised by the Act were relatively rare, with some acknowledgement of the problems that enforcement created within families. On the other hand, spending on elders was severely curtailed from the 1870s onwards, with a new drive to emphasize self-help and reliance upon the family. David Thomson (1991: 217) describes the impact of this development in the following way:

> Only by cutting assistance to all, even the welfare core, could the policy emphasizing self-responsibility be successful: so ran the argument amongst poor law and charity authorities in the last quarter of the century. If this caused misery amongst the elderly then it had to be so, in the interests of a greater good. The policy was followed with remarkable vigour. Within twenty years public spending upon the aged was cut to a third or less of what it had been in 1870. Moreover, families were pressed as a matter of course to take up financial responsibilities for the aged, and from 1870 the court records are filled with reports of prosecutions of sons, and a few daughters as well.

The impact of this change in policy is reflected in Charles Booth's researches for his study *The Aged Poor*. These provided clear illustrations of the pressures within families arising from the drive to cut welfare spending:

> In the Midlands it was reported not only that children had to be compelled to contribute, but also that they sometimes even moved away from the area 'to evade claim'. In the Eastern Counties, too: 'Quarrels frequently arise between children as regards giving the help. Parents are unwilling to ask help from children and expect little'. And from Chipping Sodbury in Gloucestershire came the comment: '[The] Aged prefer a pittance from the parish (regarded as their due) to compulsory maintenance by children; compulsion makes such aid very bitter'.
> (Horn 1976: 205–6, citing Booth 1894)

An additional impact of the new policy towards the poor was the insistence that those on relief move into the workhouse. This institution must figure prominently – directly or indirectly – in any history of abuse of older people. In Edwardian Britain, one in ten of the population aged 75 and over would end their days in the workhouse, although the fear of this possibility affected a much larger number. There can be little doubting the dreadful experience facing those forced to end their days within such institutions. Thompson *et al.* (1990: 37) summarize this as follows:

> The regime of the workhouse was deliberately deterrent, and at least up to the 1890s married couples would be forced to live apart within it. Little beyond food was provided: not even false teeth to eat with. Middle-class visitors entering a workhouse for the first time could be deeply shaken by the harsh indignity of the prison-like routine, the grotesque, despairing toothless faces, 'the forlorn, half-dazed aspect of these battered human hulks who were once young'. There was no need 'to write up the words "Abandon hope all ye who enter here"', George Lansbury wrote of the Poplar workhouse. 'The place was clean: brass knobs and floors were polished, but of goodwill, kindness there was none'.

Little wonder that Flora Thompson (1945) recalled 'tears of gratitude' running down the cheeks of people collecting their first old-age pension back in 1909. Pensions from the state offered the dual promise of release from the threat of the workhouse on the one side, and dependence on the family on the other. The reality, however, was that with the pension fixed well below subsistence level, the lives of the elderly continued to be marked by acute poverty and dependence, in many cases, on the family. This was brought out in the numerous surveys conducted from the late nineteenth century onwards, by investigators such as Booth, Rowntree and others. *The New Survey of London Life and Labour* (Llewellyn Smith 1934) found one of the principal causes of poverty to be old age, this accounting for a third of all families in poverty in the East End of London. Herbert Tout (1938), in his Bristol survey, found that if older people could not find anywhere to live rent free and had only their old-age pension on which to live, they would automatically fall below the poverty line. In the 1930s, Rowntree estimated that in York 33 per cent of old-age pensioners were living below even his own stringent poverty line. Describing their lives, Rowntree commented: 'They are, indeed, the poorest people in the city. Of course they do get an occasional ounce of tobacco, or glass of beer, but only by suffering a little more from cold and undernourishment. A poor drab ending to a life'(cited in Stevenson 1977: 81).

The pressures on older people and their families were increased in periods of economic recession. The economic depression in the 1930s undoubtedly created tensions within the households of the poor. Ellis Smith, MP, told the House of Commons in November 1938: 'Old grandfathers and grandmothers are afraid to eat too much food lest they should be taking the bread out of the mouths of their grandchildren' (cited in Branson and Heinemann 1971: 229). Another MP told of 'an old man bent and worn, who has worked in the steel industry all his life', and who had said: 'I only have 10s a week. I am living with my son, but his wife says she can no longer afford to keep me. I don't know what to do. I don't want to go to the workhouse, but there is nothing else to be done' (cited in Branson and Heinemann 1971: 229; see also Stevenson and Cook 1977).

Beyond these particular experiences, some general changes to the lives of elders are of relevance to any discussion on the history of abuse. First, there was the growth of mandatory retirement, this reinforcing the idea of older people as representing a distinctive social category (Phillipson 1993). The emergence of retirement also had the important effect of raising issues about the 'social redundancy of the old' as well as their economic dependency (given the insufficiency of state pensions). These policy changes undoubtedly created tensions within the family (Peter Townsend's (1957) description of retired men in Bethnal Green in the 1950s is a powerful indictment of the problem of the 'redundant old'); they also raised concerns about older people's broader role in society, which were reflected in debates about ageism and discrimination introduced by writers such as Robert Butler (1985).

A second development, however, was the impact of industrialization and urbanization on the social context of abuse. Here, and building on the argument outlined by Peter Stearns (1986), it is important to distinguish between the period from the late nineteenth century to the 1950s (the modern age), and the phase from the 1960s to the mid-1990s (the contemporary period). These periods represent very different contexts for older people, in terms of their relationship both within the family and with other social and political institutions. The comparison between these periods will now be sketched, with a brief summary of the implications for understanding current concerns for abuse of older people.

The social context of abuse and neglect

At the beginning of this chapter we identified the emergence of a concern with abuse in the mid-1970s, anxieties which resurfaced in the late 1980s/early 1990s. The context for these was, however, somewhat different than in the period up to the 1950s. The facts here are relatively straightforward and well documented. First, there was a build up in the size of urban households in the nineteenth century, with the augmentation of the nuclear family coming through children remaining at home for longer periods, a rising incidence of unrelated lodgers, and an increase in the co-residence of non-nuclear kin (Seccombe 1991). In terms of the last of these, older people were especially important, with an increasing tendency for women to return to live with one of their daughters following the death of their husbands. Seccombe (1993) suggests that the taking in of widows appears to have been very common, with Anderson's study of mid-nineteenth century Preston showing over 80 per cent of women 65 and over living with their children. More generally, it is the density of kinship networks which appears to be an important feature of the way many communities developed. This is clearly illustrated in post-war studies by Sheldon (1948) in Wolverhampton, Townsend (1957) in Bethnal Green, and Willmott and Young (1960) in Woodford. In Wolverhampton, in the late 1940s, one-third of older people had relatives living within a mile (four per cent with children living next door). In Bethnal Green, in the early 1950s, each older person had an average of 13 relatives living within a mile; 53 per cent of older people had their nearest married child either in the same dwelling or within five minutes; in Woodford, the figure was 40 per cent; in Wolverhampton, approaching 50 per cent.

The 1960s, however, introduced a significant break with the pattern identified above. Richard Wall (1992) in fact stresses the basic continuities in household structure over several centuries, with a marked change in living patterns only coming in the last 30 years, with the increase in those living alone, and the corresponding decline in those living with people other than their spouse. By the 1990s, five per cent of older people in Britain lived with a child, in comparison with 40 per cent at the start of the 1950s. Similar trends have been cited in the case of the United States. In 1900, more than 60 per cent of all persons aged 65 and over resided with their children. Haber and Gratton (1994: 44) observe: 'Whether as household head or as a dependent of their offspring, the elderly shared residences with the young, uniting their assets and abilities as well as their conflicts'. As in the case of Britain, improved personal resources (especially with the growth of pensions) encouraged the development of separate residences. Haber and Gratton note that the allocation of pensions brought two important trends: steep declines in complex living arrangements, and striking increases in independent, autonomous households. By 1962, the proportion of the old who lived with their children had dropped to 25 per cent and by 1975 to only 14 per cent.

At first glance these figures are difficult to reconcile with concern about abuse, given that it developed at a time when older people were becoming more dispersed and separate from immediate kin. On deeper investigation, however, it is possible to identify factors which brought to the surface awareness of the nature of abuse which had not been present in the period up to the mid-1960s. What were the key factors for each period which either limited or enhanced awareness of abuse? In terms of the first period, up until the mid-1960s, three points should be noted: first, the lack of conceptualization of the problem; second, the mediating role of the kinship network; third, the characteristics of the older population. The first of these is probably crucial in terms of the lack of definition of abuse as a distinctive social problem. This itself is bound up with the very modest standard of living which older people were seen as having a right to expect. In an important sense, a concept of abuse and neglect can emerge only when society sees the achievement of a particular standard of care as important. This was certainly not in evidence in the pre-war period, and it took some time to develop even after the war (Phillipson 1982). In the context of scares about the effects of population ageing, the possibility of the maltreatment of the old – if it was taking place – was simply not an area which had to be tackled with any urgency.

Another factor is the extent to which the social relations of older people were mediated by relatively dense kinship structures. One possibility is that these may have provided an informal check on certain types of abuse (though further research is needed to test this possibility). Equally, the external checks on family behaviour were less strong, given the absence of any professional or legislative focus on the needs of older people (a factor which undoubtedly marks this period out from the later one). A further point to consider is that the importance of kinship ran alongside a higher level of tolerance (by society at least) of domestic violence. The extent to which the latter is historically and politically constructed has been discussed by Linda George (1989: 3) in her major review of the politics of domestic violence:

> First, the very definition of what constitutes acceptable domestic violence, and appropriate responses to it, developed and then varied according to political moods and the force of certain political movements. Second, violence among family members arises from family conflicts which are not only historically influenced but political in themselves, in the sense of that word having to do with power relations. Family violence usually arises out of power struggles in which individuals are contesting real resources and benefits. These contests arise not only from personal aspirations but also from changing norms and conditions.

George's argument underlines the importance of relating elder abuse to changing social and communal norms, this creating increased concern over the past two decades for what has almost certainly been a longstanding social problem.

Finally, numbers alone may be an important part of the explanation. The group cited as the most vulnerable to abuse (those aged 75 and over), was relatively small up until the 1940s. The significant shift comes from the 1950s onwards, with the number of people aged 75 plus in Great Britain increasing from 1.7 million to nearly 4 million by the early 1990s. Very old people were, in short, numerically of much less significance, although, as Sheldon's (1948) work indicated, they could still raise pressures for the families supporting them.

Abuse in the contemporary period

In comparison, the period from the 1960s has a number of characteristics which identify the issue of abuse as a new social problem. These may be summarized in terms of: first, the concern with various forms of domestic violence; second, the pressures arising from residential separation; third, the development of new policies on community care; fourth, the growth of professional groups concerned with the care of older people; fifth, the impact of critical perspectives within social gerontology.

First, the discovery of elder abuse was part of a wider conceptualization of the pervasiveness of violence within the family (Kingston and Penhale 1994). In the earlier period, violence, although undoubtedly present and real – for women in particular – tended to be hidden from view. From the mid-1960s (and starting with the identification of child abuse) the problem of the family became a focus of concern, with the possibility of violence and maltreatment being viewed as endemic to this institution.

Second, the residential separation of elderly people itself raised pressures of different kinds. This point has been developed by Stearns (1986: 20) in the following way:

> The . . . separation of the elderly, although at first a source of conflict reduction, may have adverse consequences as well. The separation does not eliminate tight intergenerational bonds, but it may lessen their power.

It leaves the elderly more literally isolated, and so more vulnerable than before. It produces inevitable dislocation when, after a long period of separate residence, medical or economic dependency forces reintegration of an older relative into the household.

Third, attention to abuse was also assisted by the growth of community care policies (Ogg and Munn-Giddins 1993). Here, the emphasis on deinstitutionalization produced concern with, on the one side, the pressure faced by informal carers (Dalley 1988), and, on the other, the potential for neglect and inadequate care of vulnerable groups such as very elderly people. The pressure facing informal carers is certainly crucial to the debate on elder abuse, and has been a major theme in many conceptualizations of the problem (see, especially, Steinmetz 1988). However, the demographic issue which underpins this concern, that of parents living longer with fewer children to look after them, is itself relatively modern. Indeed, it is meaningful to see the 1950s as a watershed following which, on the one hand, older people were a larger proportion of the population, but where, on the other hand, they had fewer children.

Anderson (1985), in his study of the British family lifecycle from the mid-eighteenth to mid-twentieth centuries, calculates statistics relating to the ratio of survival years past 65 to children alive. The 2.3 children who reached age 25 years from the cohort of mothers born in 1891 could expect their mothers to live on average 12 years past 65, giving a ratio of mother's survival years to each surviving child of over five. By contrast, the 3.6 children reaching age 25 from the 1801 cohort of mothers had mothers who on average would die only three years after passing 65, giving a ratio of surviving years to children of less than one. Anderson (1985) concludes from these figures that the potential burden of care per child has increased significantly over the past century. This historical trend has continued from the 1950s to the present day. The implications of this development for issues relating to the abuse of older people is a question we shall return to in Chapter 5.

Fourth, in contrast to the earlier period, there is the growth in size and power of what Carroll Estes (1979: 2) describes as 'the aging enterprise' – the 'programs, organizations, bureaucracies, interest groups, trade associations, providers, industries, and professionals that serve the aged in one capacity or another'. This group became more assertive in the 1980s, and was able to push a range of issues concerning older people further up the agendas both of a number of professions and of society more generally. This was also supported by the expansion of the academic study of ageing, with findings from American research in the field of abuse influencing a number of British practitioners and academics (Phillipson and Biggs 1992; Bennett and Kingston 1993; Decalmer and Glendenning 1993).

Finally, concern with abuse and neglect was assisted by a critical debate concerning prevailing ideologies about, and services for, older people. In the earlier period, the idea of abuse was almost too shocking. Society – in the form of the welfare state – had focused on elders as one of the groups it was most concerned to shield from harm and misfortune. It was one thing that research had already revealed extensive poverty and material deprivation (Townsend and Wedderburn 1965): that at least could be explained and responded to with reforms (albeit inadequate). However, the idea of older people being subject to physical violence or financial exploitation in their own homes was difficult to accept, destroying as it did the mythology surrounding the post-war family (Seccombe 1991). By the 1980s, however, the idea of violence as endemic in society was widely accepted (Dobash and Dobash 1992), as was the view that older people were still losing out in the provision of services and support (Phillipson 1982). Added to this was the view from critical perspectives within gerontology that dependency in old age (which abuse was clearly bound up with) was not a given, but was socially structured through a range of policies and professional ideologies (Estes 1993). In this sense, the phenomenon of abuse was no longer surprising in the 1990s: it could now be explained by prevailing theories and recognized as a social fact. Developing appropriate responses was, of course, another matter.

Conclusions

This chapter has reviewed the historical transformation in attitudes and experiences regarding elder abuse and neglect. Of particular interest is the change over the post-war period: we have moved from a position where maltreatment was scarcely acknowledged (at least within the family) to one where it is now defined as a major social problem (Baumann 1989). It is possible to see this development as one where we have moved from a position where abuse and neglect are 'contained' within dense kinship structures and large-scale institutions (ex-workhouses and large psychiatric hospitals), to one where they are experienced within more fragmented kinship groupings, as well as smaller residential homes. This historical shift in the experience of abuse – if real – undoubtedly represents a challenge for those concerned with helping and supporting abusers and abused in the community. This is a theme to which we shall return later.

2

Theoretical issues

Introduction

A clear understanding of the theoretical base of debates around elder abuse can provide the researcher, the practitioner and the student of ageing with a number of conceptual tools. First, it will allow a deeper knowledge of contributory factors and the patterns underlying them. Second, understanding a number of theoretical positions will make it easier to see the advantages and disadvantages of any one theory. Third, comparison is allowed between initially tacit assumptions held by the reader and the explicit ideas that have evolved to make sense of the phenomenon. Theory thereby helps to focus personal formulations and aids the discovery of explanations that best fit with the reader's circumstances and individual beliefs. The favoured theoretical base will also shape the type of action that is felt to be most appropriate.

This chapter divides approaches to elder abuse and neglect into those that are pragmatic and those that are conceptual. Pragmatic approaches tend to arise from practice settings such as child protection and domestic violence. Conceptual approaches are drawn from existing sociological or psychological thought and applied to elder abuse and neglect along with other social problems. The chapter goes on to consider a blueprint of what an adequate theory might look like, reviewing some of the key elements which should be included. The discussion goes on to review the notion of citizenship as a means of bringing together different levels of analysis, whilst reminding us of the human and civil rights that may be denied to older people.

Theoretical perspectives

A number of attempts have been made to classify theoretical approaches to elder abuse. Aber and Zigler (1981) have distinguished between legal, care management and research definitions. Johnson (1986) classified elder abuse intervention into physical, psychological, social and legal types, these reflecting the involvement of different professional groups. In both cases, mistreatment has been approached from a pragmatic point of view, which is to say that the locus and method of intervention have been used to make sense of the problem. Other researchers have attempted to apply ideas from the study of wider social phenomena, so that elder mistreatment can be seen as a particular example of a more general conceptualization. Phillips (1986) explored the explanatory value of three psychosociological theories – situational, social exchange and symbolic interactionism – in relation to abuse and neglect. Gelles and Loseke (1993) compared psychological, sociological and feminist approaches to family violence. Phillipson and Biggs (1992) drew from social gerontology, the study of older people, to note the influence of disengagement, activity, exchange, interactionist and social construction theories on elder mistreatment. Key theories will be summarized later in this chapter; for the moment we simply want to indicate that both pragmatic and conceptual approaches will influence the way in which elder mistreatment is classified and understood.

Gelles and Loseke (1993) point out that the choice of approach or theory often reflects the background of the writers themselves. They observed a difference between what they called, first, primarily scientific and, second, social activist approaches. The former is concerned with objectivity, the accurate and disinterested study of a phenomenon, the latter with direct involvement and promoting social change in a particular direction. A scientific approach places most emphasis on facts, whilst social activism emphasizes values. One might be viewed as 'emotionally neutral', the other as biased in favour of a particular outcome. However, the study of social problems rarely conforms to these idealized positions, with most approaches including elements of both. Researchers rarely investigate areas that they do not consider to be socially important, whilst campaigners require independent information if their cause is to be taken seriously.

In what follows, pragmatic and conceptual understandings will be outlined in turn. Our own views on what an adequate understanding should embrace, and some of the consequences, will then be explored.

Pragmatic approaches

Pragmatic approaches to elder mistreatment tends to reflect the systems and organizations which have to respond to the problem. Understanding will be influenced by the history of responding to previous problems, similarities that can be seen, and the lessons drawn from that experience. The service base, the particular institutions charged with developing policies, will have their own culture and understanding of their role and expertise that will influence the boundaries put around legitimate action. Practices that have emerged will affect the way that mistreatment is defined, perceived and responded to.

Two approaches seem to have most influenced the positioning of elder abuse and neglect in the UK and North America, namely child protection and responses to domestic violence.

Elder and child protection

Child protection work has become a central concern for social welfare agencies on both sides of the Atlantic. In the case of Britain, this has led to the consolidation of statutes affecting the care of minors (the 1989 Children Act), a focus on reporting procedures, registers of families at risk, and the need for inter-professional coordination (Hallett and Birchall 1992). The guiding principle of this work has been that the 'interests of the child are paramount' (Children Act 1989). However, the precise nature of those interests rely heavily on the accumulated wisdom of professional helpers, in negotiation with parental carers.

Comparisons with child protection have been noted as holding both advantages and disadvantages for the deeper understanding of mistreatment of older people. Penhale (1993) cites research that shows similarities between these two forms of mistreatment. These would include the following:

1 transmission of violent responses across generations (see Chapter 5), so that violence is learned and copied, and is passed on from one generation to another;
2 a focus on attempts to control behaviour which is seen as difficult or problematic by the carer, rather than a focus on the victim's perspective;
3 the predominantly male nature of violence and female nature of neglect;
4 the reluctance of society to admit that family violence exists.

Phillipson and Biggs (1992) note that violence to both young and old results from an imbalance of power, deprivation of rights and liberties, and a failure to provide optimal conditions for development. Biggs and Phillipson (1994) cite the importance of multiprofessional collaboration for both groups. However, concern that elder protection should not simply be an extension of child protection services was sufficient for Department of Health (1993) guidelines to include an appendix outlining differences in familial and social context between the two populations.

Differences undoubtedly occur at a number of levels. Pillemer (1993) notes that elder abuse is less prevalent (at between 2 and 4 cases per 100 of the general population) than child abuse (at about 12 per 100, on US norms). Both Penhale (1993) and Phillipson (1994) point out that whilst children are viewed as in need of protection as a future resource, older people are stereotypically seen as burdensome. Paradoxically, the use of force as a corrective is viewed by many as an acceptable part of child-rearing, whilst similar acts towards older adults would be considered an assault. Elders, whilst often more frail than children, have more legal, emotional and economic independence by virtue of their adult status.

Over-emphasis of parallels between elder and child mistreatment may therefore eclipse the distinctive qualities of the former (Phillips 1989), a phenomenon that Glendenning (1993) links to a perceived dependence of older people and a tendency to infantilize them. Difficulties in detection and recognizing symptoms, the degree of carer optimism that a future state of independence will be achieved, and that carers of older people are often elderly, in poor health or disabled themselves, have been noted as key differences between the two populations (Penhale 1993).

Phillipson and Biggs (1992) point to significant mistakes that might be made if the child protection analogy is used to guide intervention. Whereas children are generally dependent on their carer, research has suggested that carers may be emotionally and financially dependent on the older person, a reversal of what would otherwise be expected (Pillemer and Wolf 1986). Abuse may not therefore be a consequence of the carer's burden, so much as a rebellion against a position of dependency on the victim. It gives us a clear example of the type of problem that can arise through direct analogy with child protection work. Financial abuse is virtually unknown in child care but is increasingly seen as a major form of elder abuse in the US. If elder mistreatment is seen exclusively through the lens of child protection, this and other forms of abuse would be missed.

A further point of discontinuity between child protection and elder protection arises because the latter addresses relations between adults. It cannot be assumed that professional helpers should judge what would be in the best interests of, nor take over decision making for, the vulnerable older person. Indeed, such a course of action may increase the elder's sense of powerlessness, and the possibility of additional forms of abuse. The adults involved may also share a considerable life history, including patterns of mutual dependency within a longstanding relationship. This may make it difficult to identify persons as exclusively victims or perpetrators.

So, approaches to understanding elder mistreatment can usefully build on some elements of child protection. However, intergenerational relations that exist within young families and between older people and their carers vary considerably as a result of the social construction of childhood and older age. Serious errors of judgement can take place if approaches are uncritically transferred from one to the other. The distinctive circumstances of elders in society, as victims of mistreatment and in relation to professional practice, must be acknowledged at all times.

Domestic violence

Viewing elder mistreatment as a form of domestic violence has become an increasingly popular approach, particularly in the US (Pillemer 1993; Wolf 1994). However, as Wolf notes (1994: 18), despite the fact that much elder abuse is spouse abuse, responses to the two have essentially been operating in different intellectual and organizational contexts:

> In part this separation is related to the origins of the two groups, one was a grass roots movement, anti-professional and strongly feminist, while the other was professionally motivated by social workers and nurses. In part it is also due to the original formulation of elder abuse as in caregiver stress, which certainly did not fit with the paradigm of the battered women's movement that describes the abuse as physical violence against women with children perpetrated by an oppressive husband/partner.

Morley (1994: 178) notes a similar history for the Women's Aid Movement in the UK, which has been based on local refuge groups with explicitly feminist principles of collectivism, mutual support and self-help. The relationship between professional activity and the autonomy of abused women is cast as problematic in ways that have not historically been the case in elder protection: 'Thus the dependency and control which characterise a woman's "private" relationship to her violent partner and her "public" relationships as client of professionalised bureaucracies are challenged'.

A second phase of activity surrounding domestic violence followed the release of a Home Office circular in 1990 encouraging the development of domestic violence units within police forces. The circular states that domestic violence is a crime as serious as assault by strangers. The primary duty of the police is to protect the victim and take action against the perpetrator. These developments have, as reported by Morley (1994), had a mixed effect. On the one hand, access to other services have often become limited, pending police corroboration. Police intervention, such as arrest, may increase women's vulnerability to violence through revenge, whilst removing women's control over the process of intervention (Morley and Mullander 1992). On the other, there has been an increase in local inter-agency work and resourcing for victim support schemes.

Whilst there may be historical differences concerning responses to the two issues, there is also considerable common ground. First, attempts to explain domestic violence against women have certain parallels with work on intergenerational conflict. For example, central to understanding violent relationships is, according to Goldner *et al.* (1990: 348): 'A man's attempt to reassert gender difference and gender dominance, when his terror of not being different enough from "his" woman threatens to overtake him'. (1990: 348). Similarly, a fear of dependency and personal ageing has been noted as a source of psychological conflict amongst younger people, which can become externalized when elders themselves are encountered (Knight 1986; Biggs 1993a).

Second, domestic violence can be seen as an extreme instance and reflection of wider attitudes in society towards women (Yllo 1993; Bowker 1993), a view that parallels the relationship between elder mistreatment and ageism (Butler 1987; Phillipson 1994).

Third, a domestic violence approach views the relationship between partners and formal services as problematic. For example, the growth of batterers' programmes (Adams 1988), aimed at providing therapeutic support to perpetrators, has given rise to considerable concern that primary responsibility towards the victim will be eclipsed (Morley 1994). This is reflected, to a degree, in disquiet about possible collusion between carers and professionals in cases of elder abuse (Biggs 1994).

Fourth, victims are perceived as potentially active in determining their own fate, once the threat of mistreatment is removed. This parallels research that indicates that elder abuse is not related to the dependency of the victim (Pillemer and Wolf 1986). It is also reflected in research findings that emphasize the resilience of victims, based on questionnaire responses followed up by in-depth interviews. According to Pondieks (1992: 73):

> The concept of hardiness appears to apply to the victims of elder mistreatment. They seem to have had a basic strength through which

they have found the capacity to cope or adapt, and this theme has emerged over the life course.

A domestic violence approach to elder mistreatment has, then, certain attractions over the child protection model. First, it firmly places mistreatment within the sphere of adult–adult relationships. Second, it gives emphasis to inequality of power, but sees victims as potentially active in determining their own fate. Third, it links mistreatment to the position of victimized groups in the wider society.

However, there are also certain difficulties. It was noted in the previous section that, in cases of elder abuse by informal carers, it is not always possible to define clearly a victim and perpetrator, and in longstanding relationships attention should be paid to the nature of intergenerational communication. This is in contradiction to an assertion that the status of victim and perpetrator be clearly maintained in cases of domestic violence. This point has given rise to heated debate between advocates of a 'domination' model of domestic violence (Marx-Ferree 1990; Jones and Schecter, 1992; Yllo 1993), and those who propose a 'conflict tactics' approach (Gelles and Straus 1979; Gelles 1993). The former focuses on the power exerted by male aggressors, whilst the latter sees conflict as something that is constructed and maintained by both parties. This point is related to attitudes to legal intervention, where, despite reservations about the role of the police, the predominantly feminist position on domination is generally in favour of legal protection of the victim and prosecution of the perpetrator.

A second point of departure concerns a focus on violence as the central form of mistreatment. Wolf (1994) states that physical abuse of older people constituted 19.1 per cent of a nationwide US report (Tatara 1993), and Garrod (1993) found it not to be the dominant form of abuse in his UK (Durham) study. An over-concentration on this form of mistreatment may reduce professional recognition of other types of abuse and neglect.

That the study and response to domestic violence have depended heavily on the efforts of the women's movement also means that interest has been focused specifically on violence against women. Figures for elder mistreatment concur that women are more likely to be victims and men perpetrators. The US nationwide report, for instance, found that 51.8 per cent of abusers were men and 42.5 per cent women (5.8 per cent of data were missing), whilst 66 per cent of victims were female and 33 per cent male. Garrod (1993) reported similar figures for victims in a British study. However, Wolf (1994) indicates that this figure is only marginally higher than would be expected on the basis of female elders in the general population. Garrod suggests that the findings may discount gender as a significant factor once demographic patterns are taken into account.

When these figures are seen next to the suggestion by Straus (1993) that violence by women towards men is generally under-reported in comparison with violence perpetrated by men against women, the link between gender and mistreatment in later life seems less strong.

So, a domestic violence model holds promise as a contributory explanation of elder mistreatment. However, its limited scope, in terms of type of abuse and neglect, focus on female victims, and reliance on recourse to legal action, may restrict its application to elder mistreatment (see also Chapter 8).

Conceptual approaches

Certain explanations of elder mistreatment arise not from patterns of active intervention, but from the application of theories that aim more broadly to explain social behaviour. This section will outline four theories which have been most commonly associated with the abuse and neglect of older people, namely: situational models, social exchange theory, symbolic interactionism, and the social construction of old age.

The situational model

As the name suggests, the situational explanation of elder abuse locates the causes of mistreatment in the immediate circumstances surrounding the carer–elder relationship. In particular, increasing dependency on the part of the older person is seen as the cause of mounting stress for the carer, which itself increases the likelihood of abuse taking place. As such, it draws on frustration–aggression theory (Dollard 1939), which states that aggressive behaviour results when purposeful activity is interrupted and is directed at persons perceived as thwarting the aggressor's activity. Phillips (1986) summarizes the situational variables that have been linked to abuse as: first, elder-related factors such as physical and emotional dependency, poor health, impaired mental status and 'difficult' personality; second, structural factors such as emotional strain, social isolation and environmental problems; and third, carer-related factors such as life crisis, 'burn-out' or exhaustion with caring.

Immediate situational stress featured prominently in early reports on elder abuse in the US (Maddox 1977) and the UK (Eastman 1984a). In Eastman's (1984a) study, 80 per cent of cases were considered by social service staff to be stress related. Bennett and Kingston (1993) argue that the scenario of the stressed carer was difficult to dispute because research was not available at that time to support any other conceptual framework. These early findings, based on professional opinion rather than direct elder reporting, may also be subject to age-related bias in the sense that, in terms of their lifecourse development, it is easier for professional workers to identify with carers than with older people themselves (Biggs 1994).

Further reviews of the literature (Pillemer 1986; Decalmer and Glendenning 1993; Bennett and Kingston 1993; Biggs and Phillipson 1994) suggest that situational stress is unlikely to be causal. Not all stressed carers resort to abuse. Moreover, it emerged from controlled research studies that carers' character-istics, such as previous mental illness, substance misuse and financial or emotional dependency of the abuser on the older person, were more closely associated with mistreatment. This debate is examined in more detail in Chapter 5, with particular reference to family and community care. A further problem with the situational model is that it fails to address neglect and other non-physical forms of abuse. Its explanatory value, whilst being easily understood, is therefore both limited and generally unsupported by controlled research.

Exchange theory

This model draws on the power dynamics that surround caring relationships. It proposes that all social interaction consists of an exchange of rewards and punishments, which by degree determine whether the exchange will continue or cease (Gouldner 1960; Homans 1961; Dowd 1975). For continued interaction to be maintained, social actors must perceive there to be an acceptable balance both between the positive and negative results of exchange and between the benefits that accrue to each party. Failure to achieve a balanced exchange will lead to conflict or avoidance. This model would suggest that mistreatment may be seen as a response to a breakdown in the norm of reciprocity, which 'stipulates that members of a relationship should experience equitable levels of profit and loss' (George 1986: 69). The balance of exchange would have to take into account both the actual costs incurred in a transaction, plus rewards that have been forgone. Abuse would then be a response by some carers who perceive an unacceptable loss of reward and then attempt to restore control. Neglect would occur when the carer responds to a seemingly intolerable situation with attempts to avoid it altogether. This may be accompanied by a feeling of entrapment, and by a sense that there is little to be lost by being unjust oneself (Phillips 1986).

This model has gained some empirical support (Phillips 1986; George 1986), although there are difficulties in assessing costs and benefits in intimate relationships, both over time and because they depend upon the perceptions of the actors involved. Gouldner (1960) has also stated that a norm of reciprocity requires that people should help those who have helped them in the past and should not injure those who have helped them. This formulation would appear to place sanctions on any form of mistreatment where relations have been longstanding, but may have changed over time. George (1986: 73) proposes that a norm of solidarity also exists in intimate relationships, which 'involves an intensity of commitment sufficient to over-ride the self-concerns that underpin the norm of reciprocity'.

These counter-values place doubt on the usefulness of the theoretical explanation of abuse as a result of inequitable exchange in intimate relations. The theory may have greater explanatory value where relations have already broken down to a degree that negates personal commitment, or where commitment never existed. Jack (1994) has indicated that because the care of older people often occurs in a markedly female environment, and is redolent with ageist assumptions, informal care may be significantly lacking in structural rewards. The possibility of abuse and neglect as a means of expressing powerlessness is therefore enhanced, along the lines that exchange theory would predict. George (1986) found that the use of exchange explanations of caring depended on the original relationship between carer and the person cared for. The further away relations were from an intimate relationship, for example in-laws as opposed to spouses, the more likely notions such as fairness and extrinsic reward were to be used. It has been suggested that in this type of situation an exchange model might usefully be adopted by practitioners themselves. Wolf (1992), for example, notes social exchange as a model for intervention, if rewards and punishment can be manipulated to reduce dependency on the elder and increase the cost of abuse or neglect.

Exchange theory might, then, be an appropriate means of analysing maltreatment when social interaction has either deteriorated or was not intimate at the outset. Whilst it may be considered unduly mechanistic and possibly uncritical of instrumental relations within capitalist societies, it opens the possibility, as Jack (1994) has shown, of including wider social factors in an understanding of elder abuse and neglect.

Symbolic interactionist theory

This approach places emphasis on the way that social life is created and maintained through the interactions of members of a social group (Goffman 1961; McCall and Simmons 1966; Blumer 1969). Interaction is symbolic insofar as actions are based on perceived images of the self and others, rather than any one true reality. Rather than responding to rewards and punishments, participants have goals they assume to be valid and also attribute motivations to others which may or may not correspond to what the other person intends or assumes. From this perspective, the expectations that social actors hold and the degree of agreement between their views of the world take centre stage.

Elder mistreatment would be viewed as a consequence of the systems of interaction maintained by families, institutions and other social groups. More specifically, the theory would predict that processes associated with ageing, both social and biological, might change role expectations within the system that the older person was part of. Such alterations would challenge hitherto stable identities, causing a disagreement in perceptions of behaviour and thus increase misunderstanding and role strain. This could be resolved by the negotiation of new self-validating identities and relationships. Alternatively, forms of psychological abuse, such as infantilization, could emerge, leading to other forms of abuse and neglect.

Difficulty in reconciling whom the older person was perceived to be in the past with whom they are now perceived to be might also help to explain the occurrence of abuse or neglect (Phillips 1986). If 'difficult' behaviour is regarded as being intentional, if it cannot be given an alternative meaning as part of a disability or illness, vulnerable older people might be blamed and punished.

Symbolic interactionism thus places emphasis on individual and group assumptions which then determine the likelihood of mistreatment. This considerably extends understanding of the problem in a number of directions. First, behaviour towards older people is seen as depending upon stereotypes current in social groups. Second, behaviour has to be seen as part of an ongoing process. As one part of the system changes, so will others, so that changes in the capacities of one member of a family would resonate amongst others, influencing their perceptions and attributions. Third, an emphasis on the construction of personal meaning alerts the investigator to individual differences, both in the way mistreatment is perceived and in an ability to consider alternatives. It proposes a more complex world for the practitioner, where attention has to be paid to the attitudes that maintain behaviour, considered alongside alternative options and roles that might reduce mistreatment. Its complexity is, however, problematic when it comes to determining clear hypotheses. Phillips (1986: 211) concludes that symbolic interactionism may be inaccessible to empirical testing and 'may not be able to provide the predictive power necessary to identify which families are likely to abuse and which are not'.

Social construction of old age and political economy

Both social constructionism and political economy approaches to older age constitute attempts to place ageing within a broader social context. Both are concerned with what it means to be old in contemporary Western society, how ageing is conceived, and the value attributed to that part of the lifecourse. Whilst social constructionism primarily addresses the phenomenology of everyday existence, in other words, the way that meanings are sustained between people, political economy examines the contribution of policy to how social problems are interpreted.

The social construction of reality (Berger and Luckman 1966) proposes that reality is created and maintained through social institutions that socialize their members into accepting certain definitions of behaviour as objective fact. Beliefs are therefore seen as having qualities that are both objective and external to the individual actor and subjective in that they are human products that depend upon the particular social group that actors live within and are actively maintained by them. This has given rise to the concept of a 'common-sense' reality which is taken for granted by the ordinary member of that group, and which may not be challenged until alternative cultures or institutions are encountered. When these assumptions are disrupted, a process of 'nihilation' may come into play in order to reassert the status quo. Disruptive persons or events may be given negative status, be marginalized and therefore not taken seriously; their behaviour may be reinterpreted so that their meaning can be incorporated into the existing reality. If these strategies fail, more radical solutions such as segregation and ultimately destruction of the other may be adopted.

In this context many of the influences affecting elders can be seen to reflect a political economy explanation of the position of older people in society. In other words, prejudice based on age can be seen as the product of particular divisions of labour and the structure of social inequality, rather than a natural product of the ageing process (Phillipson 1982). Walker (1980) highlighted this perspective with the notion of the 'social creation of dependency in old age'. Townsend (1981) used a similar term when he described the 'structured dependency' of older people, which is seen to arise from compulsory retirement, poverty and restricted domestic and community roles. Finally, Estes (1979: 7) coined the term 'the aging enterprise',

To call attention to how the aged are often processed and treated as a commodity and to the fact that age-segregated policies that fuel the aging enterprise are socially divisive 'solutions' that single out, stigmatize and isolate the aged from the rest of society.

Biggs and Phillipson (1994) point out that an implication of this approach is that abuse may arise from the way in which older people come to be marginalized by society, and that health and social services are not immune from this process and often reinforce the dependency created through wider social and economic trends.

Rather than challenge abuse and neglect, social institutions, such as social policy, health and welfare services and the family, may maintain it as part of their systems of common-sense understanding. This view would tend to look for longstanding patterns of behaviour in such systems which maintain abuse and may simply not recognize mistreatment as anything out of the ordinary. Further, abuse and neglect may be triggered when established roles are challenged and various forms of 'nihilation' come into play.

Whilst the authors are unaware of controlled studies addressing this hypothesis, it is possible to point to certain trends that would suggest its influence. These include the often hidden nature and resilience of forms of institutional mistreatment (Chapter 6), the collusive potential of relationships both within maltreating families and between those families and community services (Chapter 5) and the assumptions implicit in social policy towards older people in general and victims of abuse and neglect in particular (Chapter 4).

Summary

The merit of the above theories may lie in how far they are able to explain different facets of elder mistreatment, at different levels and in different circumstances. They are rarely mutually exclusive and researchers and practitioners would need to draw upon all theories identified in analysing and developing responses to mistreatment. Sprey and Matthews (1989: 58) offer helpful advice in this regard:

> The usefulness of each explanatory approach depends upon exactly what is being explained. Lines of questioning become of decisive importance in making theoretical sense of a set of events that on a surface level seem to defy meaningful categorical conceptualisation. To ask why given individuals turn into abusers or exploiters, for instance is essentially a psychological issue. To query under what conditions such persons actually abuse quite specific others requires social-psychological analysis. And to ask which attributes or familial structures may induce relations that are violent or neglect-prone is for sociologists or anthropologists to explain.

This advice is of considerable importance in maintaining a balanced debate on elder mistreatment.

A model for understanding elder abuse

Levels of analysis

In order to understand elder mistreatment it is necessary to have a framework that explains the phenomenon at a number of levels. We would suggest that an adequate explanation should be able to take at least three levels into account:

1 the social and historical context of mistreatment, in other words, how it is socially constructed;
2 the interplay of social actors within that social space, or how key figures interact with each other;
3 the way that the problem is conceived by individuals involved, and how they respond psychologically.

First, then, mistreatment must be seen in a social and historical context. This means that under certain conditions our understanding will take a particular form. Certain phenomena and relationships will be emphasized, whilst others will be seen as less important. Recognition of abuse will, for example, differ depending upon whether it takes place in a long-stay institution or in an elder's own home. The social and historical context will influence common-sense assumptions about vulnerable elders in the wider society and expectations of behaviour towards them, in other words their position in that social space. These factors will help to determine what is seen as a social problem, who the key actors are and, in some cases, whether it is seen as a problem at all (Baumann 1989).

Second, mistreatment must be understood in terms of how different participants interact within that socially constructed space. This would include the nature of the relationship to the victim, whether, for example, an abusive situation includes a professional worker or a relative, the degree to which protagonists share a common personal history and the power that one holds over another. The way that mistreatment is addressed will depend upon how different roles are negotiated. In a community setting, this may focus on the differing priorities of informal carers, the nominated victim and a social worker. In an institution it might depend upon the status of patients, the professional background of the front-line worker and the way that the workplace is managed.

Finally, the way that those involved see themselves and explain their circumstances to themselves will influence thought and feelings in response to mistreatment. It will determine which parts of the personality come into play and also the parts that are suppressed. Will professional workers act punitively or supportively, will they identify with a burdened carer (paid or unpaid) or with a victim of mistreatment? Why do the stresses of caring sometimes lead to abuse and sometimes not? Will the abused party tolerate a certain level of mistreatment because of family loyalty, accept help or see it as a threat to autonomy and freedom of choice?

The approach reviewed above would be able to make sense of common factors influencing all cases of elder mistreatment within a given society, as well as helping to interpret the special circumstances of each occurrence.

Elders and mistreatment

Awareness of the commonalities across instances of elder mistreatment will also help to distinguish it from other forms of abuse and neglect, whilst at the same time pointing towards related phenomena, in other words, what makes it special and how it is linked to other social problems. Both of these are implied by the label itself, which has two parts: it concerns elders and is to do with mistreatment.

First, the problem is construed in terms of age, and thus age-appropriate life-tasks and intergenerational relations. The specific position of older people in society, and particularly those in need of agency support, will help clarify the need to consider age as a defining variable conferring special status. This may seem obvious, but, as will be found throughout this book, will need to be elaborated if elder mistreatment is to be fully understood.

Second, mistreatment concerns the denial, either actively or passively, of fundamental human rights: to live safely and securely, to participate in society, and to maximize one's potential in accordance with personal wishes (so long as those wishes do not harm or infringe the rights of others). This second factor facilitates parallels with other groups in society who may suffer discrimination, of which mistreatment is an extreme form, and emphasizes a potentially active role for nominated victims. In order for abuse to take place, the victim must be placed outside categories of belonging that place constraints on acceptable social behaviour.

Welfare and citizenship

The commonalities noted above link elder mistreatment to the concept of citizenship. Citizenship sits at the crossroads of socially constructed meaning, interpersonal relations and definitions of self-hood. It helps define certain courses of action. It raises questions of balance between rights and obligations, participation and marginalization, coercion and consent, the individual and the collective. Moreover, citizenship is defined and redefined in accordance with the socio-economic context, the interaction between different social actors and groups, the acceptability of social behaviour towards members and non-members and, finally, the internal dynamic of the self in relation to these forces. In a formal sense, it defines the relationship between the individual and the state.

Turner (1993: 2) sees the question of citizenship structured around two main issues:

> The first concerns the nature of social membership in highly differentiated societies, where the authority of the nation state appears to be under question. The second range of issues concern the problem of efficient allocation of resources, which continue to be dominated by various forms of particularistic inequality. . . . [Citizenship is] that set of practices, juridical, political, economic and cultural, which define a person as a competent member of society, which as a consequence shape the flow of resources to people and social groups.

Phillipson (1994: 105) has extended Turner's argument, noting certain implications for elder mistreatment arising from changes to the organization of care in the community, which 'may be understood as part of this wider debate about social integration, in this instance concerning the place of groups vulnerable to the experience of marginalisation'.

Ignatieff (1989: 72) points out in this context that:

> The language of citizenship is not properly about compassion at all, since compassion is a private virtue which cannot be legislated or enforced. The practice of citizenship is about ensuring everyone the entitlement necessary for the exercise of their liberty. As a political question, welfare is about rights, not caring, and the history of citizenship has been the struggle to make freedom real, not to tie us all in the strings of therapeutic good intentions.

A redefinition of welfare services, then, their function in society, the moral attitudes that underpin them, and the resources allocated for their operation, also repositions individuals and groups in relation to the state and thus the dominant values within any one society.

This can be seen (from Chapter 1) in the change from almshouses to the workhouse that followed industrialization in the UK. It is also reflected in the breakdown in post-war consensus politics and accompanying welfare paternalism that characterized many Western societies in the 1980s and early 1990s. During this period, for example, successive British governments reduced the role of the state as a provider of services for its citizens, using the argument that market forces would make public provision more effective and efficient whilst reducing 'interference' by the state, which was said to be both resented by and intrusive to the private individual.

Individualism is latent in Western society in both benign and malignant forms. On the one hand, the value of each person's perspective may be protected against ideological force and personal choice affirmed. On the other, collective and cultural allegiances may be negated through isolating groups with common interests and ignoring imbalances of power. Individualism became defined in a certain way during the 1980s, throughout much of the Western world, and underscored a model for understanding interpersonal behaviour based on market relations. For example, once seen though the lens of the market, welfare relations became, according to Biggs (1991: 73):

> A meeting of two individuals coming together to agree a bargain on the exchange of goods and services. . . . It proposes a vision of single persons, rationally, in possession of relevant information and a cool grasp of their own motivation, finding an agreeable solution to a mutually agreed definition of need. Each then returning to their private activities. . . .

The meaning of participation was also slanted away from a democratic and towards a market analogy (Means 1992) during the 1980s. There was a change of emphasis, from participation within services to choice between potential purchases (see Chapters 4 and 6).

Barry Richards (1989: 16) has succinctly summarized the psychological motor for the 'free market':

> We can understand the demand for freedom in the market as a narcissistic refusal to accept the boundaries of the self and be prepared to negotiate one's needs with those of others. While critics of the market lament the isolated individual bereft of community, pro-marketeers celebrate the omnipotently free individual unfettered by binding forms of relatedness to others.

This somewhat lopsided sanctioning of forms of interpersonal relations, participation and intrapsychic dynamic provides a way of understanding how individualism, as a motif for interpreting citizenship, affects welfare relationships. Citizens are seen as entering into a number of binary and essentially instrumental relationships between purchasers and providers, the common coin of exchange being the preservation of independence and the relative denial of dependency or interdependence. Thus, to be an active player in the market game the citizen must emphasize those parts of themselves that enhance a lack of dependence on others. However, as each individual also has strong dependency needs, whether or not this socially constructed reality allows their expression, it is legitimate to ask what happens to parts that cannot legitimately be expressed. There must be some place or person onto which these unacceptable, yet psychically alive, attributes can be projected. As Biggs argues (1994: 139):

> The shadow side of individualism forms a group of attributions that are particularly dangerous to welfare . . . failed individualism. . . . It is located within those who by choice or circumstance are dependent on others for the basic necessities of social survival, are demonstrably not in control of their own destinies and, by dint of that material reality, are unable to maintain a fantasy of autonomy and independence.

Thus, by sleight of hand, an emphasis on individualistic citizenship places those who need health and welfare services somewhere outside social membership. It lays the ground for placing vulnerable older people outside the circumference of what it is to be human. Once this marginality is established, social isolation, the low status attributed to elders and their services, poverty and poor quality of life for them and their carers make abuse and neglect permissible. It allows elder mistreatment to be recognized as a social problem, *and* for society to do nothing about it.

Citizenship also implies the notion of a contract between the state and the individual in society which goes something like: 'you care about our welfare and we'll play along with your definition of society'. At least in the public sphere, this goes some way to ensure the maintenance of consent and the endurance of a dominant social order. If this tacit agreement is undermined, social policy decision making can slide away from consent towards coercion. The debate changes from a concern for rights and begins to turn upon the obligations that citizenship entails. This may take the form of moral panic over the breakdown of family responsibility, the perceived unwillingness of younger generations to provide for older citizens and the consequent need to 'police' familial obligation (see Chapter 5). A reduced focus on the requirements of the end-user is complemented by increased scrutiny of the public purse. The ethics of administrative accountability may gain ground against the priorities of clinical professionalism, with an accompanying reduction of universal eligibility and increased targeting of resources to particular groups (see Chapters 4 and 5).

Intervention against elder abuse then evidences tension between a 'hands off' approach to the private sphere, in particular to family and private enterprise, and a need to inspect and ensure that obligations are being met. Tension also occurs between the resources available to support caring tasks and an increased refinement of what it means to be abused.

The way that citizenship is construed has led to a repositioning of its relation to the welfare state. It can now be seen that seemingly distant relations between social policy, institutional culture, interpersonal relations and self-perception are, in fact, closely entwined.

Elder mistreatment and citizenship

Citizenship as defined in relation to elders and to abuse helps to clarify a positive state against which mistreatment, at whatever level it occurs, can be compared. This inevitably leads to a number of moral judgements.

Citizenship would require that people be conceived as active participants in society, who, according to their ability, contribute to the definition of their own circumstances, albeit often on grounds not of their choosing. Mistreatment would imply that elders are ascribed a passive role in relation to protective services in particular and to the priorities of younger adults in general. Self-definition of one's circumstances would be severely restricted, as would the achievement of personal potential.

In terms of citizenship, certain rights would be recognized as common to all, and would not be rationed or disqualified on the grounds of age or disability.

Circumstances in which rights had been eroded or had been rationed according to age and disability would form the basis of any definition of abuse. Denial of the basic requirements for a life free from physical and sexual violence, financial exploitation and social and psychological harassment would form an opposite to a required, positive state of citizenship. Neglect would refer to exclusion from positive benefits associated with participation in society, including sustenance, social contact, physical care and psychological respect. A consequence of this perspective is that both nominated victims and perpetrators may have suffered an erosion of citizenship.

The personal requirements of each citizen in an abusive relationship would contribute to multiple understandings of that situation, and these perspectives would need to be negotiated.

Mistreatment would include the domination of requirements as defined by one party and the suppression of competing perspectives. No meaningful forum for reconciling differences would be allowed to exist, and conflict of interest would be resolved through force.

Relationships reproduce themselves under certain social and historical circumstances that might enhance or obscure a willingness or ability to see the humanity in others. However, enhanced empathy and self-activity are seen as an essential ingredient in order to reduce marginalization and stereotyping. Most notably, these relationships would be played out in relation to health and welfare settings, where tensions arise between public and private culture, communication between generations and the competing requirements of service users, and formal and informal carers.

The perspective on elder mistreatment proposed here would suggest that:

1 Elder mistreatment achieves the status of a social problem under circumstances in which a previously socially constructed reality is in transition.
2 Recognition of abuse differs from its actual occurrence and the nature of recognition will vary over time and context.
3 Professional interactions and perspectives will determine how abuse is conceived and how responses are made, rather than the nature of the abuse itself.
4 The abuser's circumstances and capacities will determine whether mistreatment occurs to a greater degree than the individual characteristics of the victim.
5 Certain social contexts contain factors that facilitate abusive behaviour and thus make it more likely that particular forms of abuse will occur rather than others.

Conclusions

A number of approaches have been taken to understanding elder mistreatment, which have been categorized as either pragmatic or conceptual in origin. Pragmatic approaches tend to reflect other forms of protection work, and may not be adopted as models for elder abuse without significant modification. Conceptual approaches often reflect the extension of a general theory to this particular social problem. They thus tend to lose explanatory value in proportion to an inability to take the particular circumstances of older people into account.

If theoretical understanding of elder mistreatment is to progress, it needs to take cognisance of the interaction between at least three levels of analysis. These would include the social and historical construction of mistreatment, interpersonal relations between key social actors, and their personal conceptions and responses.

Further, specific attention would need to be paid to both the unique characteristics of mistreatment as it affects older people, and general characteristics which link explanations to wider social issues.

An attempt has been made to begin this task, using the motif of citizenship in older age to explore the nature of elder mistreatment as a social problem, its location within changing social institutions, and the consequences for relations between social actors in that space.

3

Definitions and risk factors

Introduction

The issue of defining elder abuse has raised a number of problems and difficulties for researchers and practitioners alike. In the 1980s, a range of definitions emerged from the American literature, although many of these were viewed as lacking both clarity and precision (Bennett and Kingston 1993). In part, this reflected the way in which investigators combined a range of perspectives when assessing the area of abuse: the victim, the carer, the social worker, the nurse (Glendenning 1993). The result was a lack of focus in the definitions which eventually emerged.

This chapter will review some of the approaches to defining abuse. It will also consider evidence concerning the amount of abuse and neglect in the community. Finally, the issue of risk factors for abuse will be explored, with a range of research studies being reviewed and analysed.

The development of definitions

It is important to recognize that elder abuse is a complex phenomenon, and that there is no 'uniform, comprehensive definition of the term' (Johnson 1986: 168). Definitions are, however, important for several reasons. First, as pointers towards the social problem in question, they guide the enquirer towards a clearer understanding of what the issue involves. Second, definitions help to focus on the social problem in question and differentiate that specific area of concern from other phenomena. Third, definitions are also necessary to guide professionals and permit intervention.

Critical analysis of definitions is also necessary because the debates have been restricted to abuse in the family setting, with a modest amount of work in institutional or special settings. The entire field of family violence has also been under-developed and this is reflected in the elder mistreatment debate.

Early terminology

Since the first British reference to 'granny battering' (Baker 1975), terminology has changed considerably in both the UK and the US. The following list denotes the chronological development of terminology in the field of elder abuse and neglect:

 1 granny battering (Baker 1975);
 2 elder abuse (O'Malley *et al.* 1979);
 3 elder mistreatment (Beachler 1979);
 4 the battered elder syndrome (Block and Sinnott 1979);
 5 elder maltreatment (Douglass *et al.* 1980);
 6 granny bashing (Eastman and Sutton 1982);
 7 old age abuse (Eastman 1984);
 8 inadequate care of the elderly (Fulmer and O' Malley 1987);
 9 granny abuse (Eastman 1988);
10 mis-care (Hocking 1988).

It would seem that the term elder abuse has managed the test of time and now appears in most publications and research articles on the topic, as well as featuring in the title of the Department of Health Social Services Inspectorate report *Confronting Elder Abuse* (1992). The pressure group formed under the auspices of Age Concern England also uses the same nomenclature, Action on Elder Abuse. Nevertheless, tensions still exist over the use of satisfactory terms. For example, health and welfare providers are writing policies for 'vulnerable adults' without differentiating between people aged 18–65 and people over 65 years. Professionals with 'claims' on abuse directed towards people with learning disabilities are also expanding the definitional debate through a number of publications (Brown and Craft 1989; ARC/NAPSAC 1993). The debate will continue as new research findings appear and different pressure groups with vested interest emerge.

Early definitions

Beginning in the late 1970s, a number of definitions of elder abuse emerged. These early attempts relied heavily on elaboration of specific categories of abuse. A typical breakdown of behaviours falling into each category would include (Wolf and Pillemer 1989):

1 **physical abuse** – the infliction of physical harm, injury, physical coercion, sexual molestation and physical restraint;
2 **psychological abuse** – the infliction of mental anguish;

3 **material abuse** – the illegal or improper exploitation and/or use of funds or materials;
4 **active neglect** – the refusal or failure to undertake a care-giving obligation (including a conscious and intentional attempt to inflict physical or emotional stress on the elder);
5 **passive neglect** – the refusal or failure to fulfil a caring obligation (excluding a conscious and intentional attempt to inflict physical or emotional distress on the elder).

The earliest definitions included specific behaviours linked to each category of abuse which show some degree of congruence with Wolf and Pillemer's (1989) typology:

1 Block and Sinnott (1979)
  Physical abuse: malnutrition, injuries such as bruises, sprains, dislocations, abrasions or lacerations.
  Psychological abuse: verbal assault, threat fear, isolation.
  Material: theft, misuse of money or property.
  Medical abuse: withholding medication or aids required.
2 Lau and Kosberg (1979)
  Physical abuse: direct beatings, withholding personal care, food, medical care, lack of supervision.
  Psychological abuse: verbal assaults, threats, provoking fear, isolation.
  Material abuse: monetary or material theft or misuse.
  Violation of rights: being forced out of one's own dwelling or forced into another setting.
3 Eastman (1982)
  The abuse, physical, emotional or psychological, of the elderly by a care-giving relative on whom that elderly person is dependent.

It is also possible to list indicators of abuse. However, it is very difficult to diagnose physical mistreatment; linking a bruise to mistreatment, for example, would require more evidence than the injury alone. The following are examples of some of the indicators that should raise a 'high index of suspicion', especially if the explanation for the acquisition of the injury does not fit the presentation (based on Bennett and Kingston 1993):

1 Indicators of physical abuse
  - unexplained bruises and welts on the face, lips, mouth, torso, back, buttocks, thighs, in various stages of healing, clustered, forming regular patterns;
  - reflecting shape of article used (cord, buckle);
  - on several different surface areas of the body;
  - regularly appear after absence, weekend or holidays;
  - unexplained burns, from a cigar or cigarette, especially on soles, palms, back or buttocks;
  - immersion burns (sock-like on feet, glove-like on hands, doughnut shaped on buttocks or genitalia;

- patterned like electric burner, iron, rope burns on arms, legs, neck, torso;
- unexplained fractures to skull, nose, facial structure, in various stages of healing;
- multiple or spinal abrasions;
- unexplained lacerations or abrasions to mouth, lips, gums or eyes, to external genitalia.

2 Indicators of sexual abuse
- difficulty in walking or sitting;
- torn, stained or bloody underclothing;
- pain or itching in genital area;
- bruises or bleeding in external genitalia, vaginal or anal areas;
- venereal disease.

An additional term to emerge was that of 'inadequate care'. Fulmer and O'Malley (1989: 21) defined this as 'actions of a caretaker that creates unmet needs for the elderly person', and defined neglect as 'the failure of an individual responsible for care-taking to respond adequately to established needs for care'. Fulmer and O'Malley's (1989) rationale for using inadequate care was pragmatic. They argued that it is easier to reach consensus on what is considered adequate (or inadequate) care than what is sanctioned as acceptable behaviours within families. In addition, health and welfare professionals would be less reluctant to use the description 'inadequate care' than define the interaction as abuse or neglect, with the emotive implications carried by the latter.

In an attempt to reach a degree of consensus in respect of defining abuse, Johnson (1986) suggested that the issue could be approached through four sequential stages:

stage 1   state of self- or other-inflicted suffering unnecessary to the maintenance of the quality of life of the older person;

stage 2   identified as one or more behavioural manifestations, categorized as physical, psychological, sociological, or legal;

stage 3   measured by determining the intensity and density of the behavioural manifestations;

stage 4   treated on the basis of whether the cause is the result of passive neglect, active neglect, passive abuse, or active abuse.

This early work has been modified and it is now claimed that there are certain critical elements to any definition for elder mistreatment. Johnson (1991: 23) uses the term mistreatment as an 'umbrella' definition, suggesting that 'elder abuse and neglect are methods of mistreatment, not conditions'; the essential components have been summed up as: 'what, how, against whom, by whom and where'. The questions to be considered should therefore include:

1 What type of behaviour?
2 How was the abuse precipitated?
3 Who was the victim?

4 Who was the precipitator?
5 Where did the abuse take place?

The extent of abuse and neglect

Discussions about the prevalence and incidence of abuse also raise a number of difficulties. To ask how much abuse there is in a given population (prevalence), and how many new cases are entering that population (incidence), is to raise questions of considerable complexity. The preceding sections would suggest some disagreement in terms of how abuse is defined. If different agencies use different definitions, figures on the extent of abuse have to be treated with some caution. Moreover, the source of information is important: are the reports from victims or are they from the records of professionals? Both raise different kinds of problems: the former issues of recall and accuracy; the latter problems of selectivity and the possibility of bias towards particular kinds of cases (Phillipson and Biggs 1995).

Accepting these points, there have been a limited number of prevalence studies in America, Canada, Britain, Finland and Australia (Pillemer and Finkelhor 1988; Podnieks, 1992; Ogg and Bennett 1992; Kivela *et al.* 1992; Kurrle *et al.* 1992). The Boston study of Pillemer and Finkelhor (1988) involved interviews with around 2,000 older people and focused on three types of maltreatment–physical abuse, verbal aggression, and neglect. The interview schedule was divided into abuse and neglect, with two subcategories of abuse: physical and psychological. The physical abuse category was operationalized using the Conflict Tactics Scale (Straus 1979). This scale uses three sets of behaviours that may be used within families to resolve conflicts: the use of reasoning, verbal or non-verbal acts that 'symbolically hurt the other', and physical force. In this survey, if an admission was made that anyone in the subject's family or close social network had been violent towards them since becoming 65, they were placed in the physical abuse category.

Psychological abuse was rated as repeated insults and threats, forming a category of 'chronic verbal aggression'. If respondents had been insulted, sworn at or threatened more than ten times in the preceding year, they were placed in the psychological abuse category. Neglect was defined as having any one of ten activities of daily living withheld by a close family member more than ten times in the preceding year.

Slightly more than 3 per cent of the population aged 65 years and over had been mistreated: 20 cases per 1,000 were physically mistreated; 11 per 1,000 were psychologically abused; and 4 per 1,000 were neglected. The authors estimate that if a national survey produced similar results, these numbers would represent almost a million people in the US. The survey also showed that spouse abuse was more prevalent (58 per cent) than abuse by adult children (24 per cent), that there were roughly equal numbers of male and female victims, and that economic status or age was not related to risk of abuse.

A national survey on elder abuse in Canada has been reported by Podnieks (1992). Data were collected through a random sample telephone survey of

2,008 elderly persons living in private dwellings. The survey uncovered 80 persons who had been maltreated according to one or more of the study criteria. For the study sample, this translated into a rate of 40 maltreated elderly per 1,000 population. Material abuse emerged as the most widespread form of maltreatment in the survey, with a prevalence rate of between 19 and 33 victims per 1,000. Chronic verbal aggression was the next most prevalent, affecting from 8 to 18 persons per 1,000. The rate for physical violence was 3 to 9 cases per 1,000, and for neglect, 2 to 6 per 1,000.

The survey in Britain by Ogg and Bennett (1992) reported on results of structured interviews (through the nationwide Office of Population Censuses and Surveys omnibus survey) with almost 600 people aged 65 and over and 1,366 adult members of households in regular contact with a person of pensionable age. One in 20 older people reported some kind of abuse, but only one in 50 reported physical abuse. Although ten per cent of adults admitted to verbal abuse, only one per cent acknowledged physical abuse.

The above studies give substantial evidence for the existence of abuse. Nevertheless, there are strong reasons to suggest that they are likely to be underestimates of the true number of victims of abuse and neglect. For example, in relation to the British study by Ogg and Bennett (1992), the following points may be noted. First, it is probable that frail and impaired elders, who could be most vulnerable to abuse, were under-represented in the sample population. Second, the nature of the responses of the 1,366 adults aged 16 and over asked whether they abused an older person must be questioned. Of the respondents, 129 (9 per cent) acknowledged verbally abusing someone of pensionable age and 12 (0.9 per cent) physically abusing an elder. It is apparent from research data that when 'sensitive topics' (Lee and Renzetti 1990) are explored, considerable ethical difficulties are experienced (Bennett and Kingston 1993). Not least is the fact that research respondents often reply to sensitive issues in a 'socially respectable' manner, thus denying the magnitude of the problem. The third issue relates to the 593 older people who responded to the survey, with 32 (5 per cent) reporting being a victim of verbal abuse, 9 (2 per cent) reporting being physically abused, and 9 (2 per cent) a victim of financial abuse. It is again highly likely that these are under-reports from the total population, given that US research suggests that victims tend not to report abuse and neglect (Tomita 1982).

All of the studies quoted are at least indicative of the existence of abuse. On the other hand, the figures – as most of the authors of such studies admit – do need to be treated with some caution. Questions have to be asked about the methods of even the more rigorous research represented in the above studies. The American and Canadian work relied either wholly or in part on telephone surveys: some types of abuse may be under-reported using this type of approach. Finally, as already argued, some groups of older people are almost certainly under-represented in the surveys – the very frail, the disadvantaged, people from minority ethnic groups. These groups may show a different pattern of abuse and neglect. Nonetheless, all three studies confirm the reality of abuse in the lives of significant numbers of older people.

Sprey and Matthews (1989) have suggested, that whether three per cent or six per cent or ten per cent of all persons over 65 are abused is largely irrelevant in practice terms. They argue (Sprey and Matthews 1989: 61): 'What must be known is who and where they are, and equally important, which forms of elder–elder and elder–other relationships are most likely to be associated with *what* types of mistreatment or neglect'. It is to the question of risk, and the factors affecting it, that we now turn.

The characteristics of the abused and abuser

The issue of who is at risk of abuse and neglect has attracted a number of research studies. Both the prevalence studies carried out by Pillemer and Finkelhor (1988) and Podnieks (1992) identified some important characteristics of abused elders. First, victims tend to be in poor health. Second, abused elderly people were more likely to be living with someone else. Third, neglected elders were most likely to have no one to turn to for support.

The Boston research, as already noted, reported that 58 per cent of the perpetrators were spouses. The underlying dynamic, as outlined by Pillemer and Finkelhor (1988), is that an elderly person is most likely to be abused by the person with whom he or she lives. Many more elders live with their spouses than with their children and thus many more elders are abused by spouses.

Additional information on the characteristics of abused older people is provided by the Three Model Project (of which the Boston prevalence study was one element), a detailed examination of elder abuse supported by the US National Institute on Aging. Bennett (1990) reports that in the three years of work of this project, 328 substantiated cases of abuse were assessed. The victims were more likely to be female, average age 76, living in a house with spouse or family. The abused were functionally impaired, half of them requiring supportive devices for mobility, a few were bedridden, a large majority had difficulties with some activities of daily living, and one-half had a cognitive impairment. The perpetrators tended to be sons rather than other family members and psychological abuse tended to be the most common type, followed by physical abuse.

The perpetrators were more likely to be dependent on the victims for finances. Their lives were stressful and they had health and financial problems. One-third had psychological problems and even more a history of mental illness and alcohol abuse. They tended to have unrealistic expectations of the capability of the abused elders and viewed their demands for attention as unreasonable.

The Three Model Project also included the study of 42 physically abused elders with a similar number of non-abused elders acting as a control group. Five hypothetical risk factors were tested in this study.

Risk factor 1: intra-individual dynamics/psychopathology

The first risk factor tested the hypothesis that mental health problems and alcohol abuse (termed intra-individual dynamics or psychopathology) was correlated with abusive behaviour. The abused elderly reported substantially higher levels of mental health or emotional problems on the part of the carer

(79 per cent v. 24 per cent). The abusers were also considerably more likely to be alcohol dependent than the carers of the non-abused group (45.2 per cent v. 7.1 per cent).

Risk factor 2: intergenerational transmission of violence

This risk factor was based on questions to the groups about the tendency to punish their children in the past. No significant difference was found between the two groups. Pillemer (1993) suggests that this method may be inadequate to gain the required details about previous intergenerational violence. It has been suggested (Bennett and Kingston 1993: 18) that the traditional view that children who were abused would seek revenge on their parents in later life cannot as yet be justified by the research data.

Risk factor 3: dependency

This particular risk factor tested the common (yet not tested) hypothesis that:

Increased dependency → stress → abuse/neglect

In this case control study the elders who were abused were *not* considered more functionally disabled and ill than the non-abused group. Furthermore, in certain areas the abused were *less* impaired than the control group. The important question now within the dependency debate concerns the notion of the abuser being dependent on the victim financially and for accommodation.

Risk factor 4: stress

External stress did not seem to be a risk factor and only three stressors appeared in the data: someone moving in with the abuser; someone leaving the household; someone getting arrested. Pillemer (1986) notes that if these three questions were not considered, stress would not be a factor of significance.

Risk factor 5: social isolation

Fewer of the abused group in the study had contacts, family and friends than in the non-abused group (36 per cent v. 17 per cent). The abused group also suggested that more of their relationships were unsatisfactory (39 per cent v. 20 per cent).

The only UK case control study is the work of Homer and Gilleard (1990). Their research questioned the stereotypical frail, white-haired woman over 75 years being abused by a well meaning daughter driven to breakdown by stress. They also suggest that abuse and neglect arise for differing reasons, and it is important to consider the characteristics of the abuser in these situations. Certainly, alcohol consumption was greater in the abuser group, and in situations of verbal abuse this behaviour appeared to have been a longstanding problem. Homer and Gilleard (1990) conclude:

It is difficult to correlate abuse with physical signs (bruising). Social isolation and lack of services did not appear to be a risk factor. There is no correlation between abuse and dementia or mental impairment. The presence or absence of disruptive behaviours seems a potential risk factor. Past abusive relationships may [also] be a risk factor.

A Swedish study by Grafstrom *et al.* (1993) compared two groups of older people, one a case study group of 219 cognitively impaired elderly; the other a control group of 255 cognitively healthy elderly. Twenty-six family members in the case study group reported abusive behaviour in the care of the elderly at home. These were compared with 154 family members in the control group who reported coping strategies that were not abusive. Amongst the families committing abuse, family members were older and judged their own health as 'worse than expected'; they also reported a 'high use of somatic and psychotropic drugs' relative to non-abusive families. Additionally they described their own psychological and physical stress as higher than the control group families. Grafstrom *et al.* (1993: 253) conclude that:

> The elderly . . . [who were] . . . reported to be abused and their carers were lonely and isolated. They had lost their social contacts, and they felt socially limited to a high degree, compared with the control group. They also complained of conflicts with their own families and friends and of limitation in their social life.

The case control study completed by Anetzberger *et al.* (1994: 188) compared 23 agency-identified perpetrators of physical abuse against elderly parents with 39 adult caring children without a history of abuse. The results suggest that alcohol use and abuse were: 'more evident among the elder abusers than non abusers, abusers were twice as likely as non abusers to have drunk alcohol . . . during the last 2 years. They also tended to drink more frequently and heavily.'

Rosalie Wolf (1989), summarizing American research on the characteristics of abused and abuser, suggests that three different profiles have emerged.

1 Victims of physical abuse and psychological abuse tend to be physically well (reasonable activities of daily living scores) but have emotional problems. The abusers have a history of alcoholism and/or mental illness, live with the victim, and are dependent upon him or her financially.
2 Victims of neglect are usually very old, and mentally and physically impaired with little social support. The carer finds the victim a source of chronic, continuing stress.
3 Victims of financial (material) abuse tend to be unmarried with limited social contacts/networks. The abusers have financial problems sometimes traceable to a history of drug or alcohol abuse.

These profiles must be regarded as somewhat tentative in the light of what is still a limited research base, drawn almost exclusively from the US. The focus on the abuser having a history of social and emotional problems is controversial and may be relevant for only a proportion of those cases involving physical abuse. Moreover, it is important to consider those contexts which might trigger abuse and neglect. For an understanding of these it is clear that sociological as well as psychological explanations of behaviour are necessary.

Finally, the research considered thus far can be most accurately described as examining abuse as it occurs in domiciliary settings. If taken on its own, it might lead to the conclusion that abuse is exclusively located within families, between carers and vulnerable older people. Other settings that are potential sites of abuse would be ignored. It is then a relatively short step to 'solve' the problem by 'rescuing' victims by placing them in a residential setting. That the family is not the sole, or even the primary, location of abuse is clear when the evidence for institutional abuse is reviewed in Chapter 6.

Synthesis of the research on risk factors

A synthesis of the data presented identifies three factors that emerge from much of the research in relation to risk and the characteristics of the abused and abuser:

1 intra-individual dynamics (psychopathology of the abuser);
2 dependency and exchange relationships;
3 social isolation.

Intra-individual dynamics

Clear evidence of either mental health problems or alcohol use and abuse is found in the work of Bristowe and Collins (1989), Pillemer (1986), Homer and Gilleard (1990) and Anetzberger *et al.* (1994). However, as Anetzberger *et al.* have pointed out, other research questions arise from the discovery of alcohol abuse as a risk factor, and these include:

1 Does alcohol render individuals prone to abuse by its ability to remove inhibitions and increase impulse response, including aggression?
2 Does prolonged alcoholism foster a dependency between adult children and their elder parents, which distresses and disturbs both, leading to the occurrence of abuse?
3 Do individuals with tendencies towards alcoholism turn to increased alcohol consumption in an attempt to cope when frustrated with elder care?

Inter-generational transmission of violence. The research evidence for this much quoted risk factor is extremely tentative, and as a risk factor does not appear in any of the case control studies. What does appear to be a risk factor is a longstanding abusive relationship that continues into later life, sometimes with 'inverted abuse', that is, women who have been victims of abuse now caring for an impaired husband and taking revenge. In the study by Grafstrom *et al.* (1992), one wife remarked 'that her husband had been an evil husband, now she was paying him back', another wife complained about being abused herself, and a third wife told about 'sexual demanding behaviour of the husband throughout their lives'. In a recent paper, exploring transmission theory, MacEwen (1994: 363) suggests that: 'simply having been exposed to aggression does not mean one will automatically become an abuser. There are other features of the original learning situation that must be considered.' With that caveat in mind, it may be pertinent at this time to suggest that although intergenerational transmission of violence cannot be stated as a risk factor, 'graduated domestic violence' perhaps can.

Dependency

Dependency as a risk factor has caused persistent controversy. However, from the case control studies, it is not at all clear that the victims of abuse are dependent on their abusers. More to the point, there is evidence that victims are less impaired than non-abused individuals, and that the abusers are often dependent on the victim (Pillemer 1986).

Stress. The risk factor of psychological stress is closely linked to dependency and appears as a factor only in the work of Grafstom *et al.* (1992). Pillemer's (1986) reference, is by contrast, to external stressors, rather than subjective notions of stress. Elder dependency and carer stress do not appear to discriminate between abusive and non-abusive groups.

Social isolation

The evidence supporting social isolation is mixed, with two studies suggesting that no evidence exists (Phillips 1983; Homer and Gilleard 1990), and two studies suggesting that social isolation is a risk factor (Pillemer 1986; Grafstrom *et al.* 1992). These findings are interesting because only Grafstrom *et al.* used a general population study. Phillips' sample was drawn from the active case loads of public health nurses, Homer and Gilleard's group were receiving respite care, and Pillemer's population was drawn from elder abuse intervention projects. The interesting question is why Pillemer's population were isolated, when the sample was drawn from elder abuse intervention projects. It is conjectured that the isolation was family and community isolation, not isolation from professionals. Further research differentiating between family/ community isolation and professional isolation, and replication studies in particular, may shed light on these conflicting results.

Conclusions: elder abuse as a social problem

This chapter illustrates the importance of a critical approach to understanding both definitions of abuse and the risk factors which make people vulnerable to abuse. At one level, some of the questions raised seem unnecessarily technical:

surely, it might be argued, do we need to be so concerned with definitions when people, in the real world, are being subject to different forms of suffering and neglect? Isn't action the key point to stop such abuse from occurring? Clearly, action is important and we shall review a number of interventions in Chapter 8. But, and here we come back to a point made in Chapter 2, intervention must be guided by a framework of some kind, one which sets out what kind of actions need to be challenged; and, from the point of view of prevention, what kind of risks create and sustain particular forms of abuse.

A rigorous approach to defining abuse is important for other reasons. First, the area of family violence in general, and elder abuse in particular, is a disputed territory in terms of the claims made by different groups in society at different points in time. Claims are made about who is doing the abuse; about the need for more resources to tackle the problem; and even about the position of older people in society. Questions of this complexity clearly need a careful and considered response; clear definitions can help and assist in this process.

A second observation might be that controversy and disagreement are to some extent to be expected in the formative years of trying to understand a new, or rediscovered, social problem. The conceptualization of any new social problem is always fraught with difficulties and elder mistreatment is not an exception to this rule. It could be argued that defining elder mistreatment will be more complicated than defining child abuse and domestic violence, because of attempts by theorists and practitioners to compare and contrast elder abuse with other phenomena (Utech and Garrett 1992; Penhale 1993). There are also the difficulties of trying to view elder abuse as a distinct and uniquely different form of family violence (Bennett and Kingston 1993: 45). Practitioners from health and social care backgrounds are aware of the child abuse and domestic violence debate, and it is therefore very easy to draw analogies from these two other areas of concern when the two phenomena may have few, or no, congruent features with elder abuse.

A third factor which suggests the need for clarity is reflected in one of the major reasons underlying the 'discovery' of elder abuse: the idea that there is something wrong in certain caring relationships. Emerson and Messinger (1977: 121) have expanded the notion of 'something being wrong' and coined the term 'troubles'. They further suggest that:

> problems originate with the recognition that something is wrong and must be remedied. Trouble in these terms involves both definitional and remedial components. Some state of affairs is experienced as difficult, unpleasant, irritating and unendurable.

The obvious difficulty has been in defining 'what is wrong' in caring relationships; hence the argument over the role of stress and dependency as risk factors in abuse. Concern has also been shown by organizations representing abused elders, especially when it was suggested that large numbers of elders may be at risk from carers. One issue here is that we must avoid trying to use the debate on elder abuse as a substitute for a wider discussion about the pressures placed upon carers of all kinds, and on the rules which govern caring in our society (see Chapter 9). A key determinant of this process is the way that social policy shapes, and is shaped by, public understanding of elder abuse and neglect. This theme will be expanded in the next chapter.

4

Social policy

Introduction

This chapter outlines the different policy initiatives that have occurred in Western countries as elder abuse has emerged as a recognized social problem. It begins by reviewing developments in the US which have shaped initiatives in other countries. The lessons on social policy that might be learned from this most developed experiment in formulating responses to elder mistreatment are considered. Sections have also been devoted to Australasia and Europe, plus a more detailed consideration of social policy in the UK.

Social policy and elder abuse and neglect in the US

In the late 1970s the US became the first country to address social policy on elder abuse and neglect. This was at a time when the UK was only beginning to consider child abuse and domestic violence as significant issues. The US policy response can be seen in retrospect to have been somewhat rapid, with the early debates focusing on the idea of criminalization. However, this is not to say that recognition was easy to achieve in trying to force federal legislation through Congress. Difficulties in the early 1980s were twofold: first, fiscal problems emerged with economic difficulties in the US; and second, the congressional view was that family matters were for the states to deal with, not the federal government. The development of a social policy response therefore took the form of state, not national, policy formulation and was inevitably fragmentary. It was necessary to wait for re-authorization of the Older Americans Act, in 1992, before a national policy on elder abuse was legislated. The resulting position has thus been subject to a number of influences over a considerable time period and, as Wolf (1994: 11) reports 'The 50 states, the Congress and the media have been the critical players in shaping the response to elder abuse in the United States.'

There is little doubt that American society currently has the highest profile on elder abuse in the developed world. As early as 1981, a Harris poll indicated that 79 per cent of the public believed elder mistreatment to be a serious problem and that 72 per cent believed it to be a major responsibility assumed by government.

It is worth examining in more detail how this level of awareness was achieved. Interest was first generated amongst the social welfare and research community and this prompted a number of investigatory projects. Second, intense media interest stimulated public debate and moral panic about the challenges of an ageing population. One of the main focus areas became elder abuse and neglect. These two factors, early research reports and media interest, prompted considerable attention from elected government representatives and plans for national elder abuse legislation were immediately considered. The high profile nature of elder abuse in the US, at least in comparison with the UK, led to state legislative intervention on a rather grand scale, culminating in all states having some form of legislation by 1988. Forty-three states enacted mandatory reporting laws and the remaining states operate systems which are not mandatory or state-wide in scope (American Public Welfare Association/ National Association of State Units on Aging 1986).

Early federal initiatives

United States federal activity in the arena of elder abuse started in 1978, with two research grants being awarded through the Department of Health and Human Services, and a special investigation by the Select Committee on Aging of the US House of Representatives. In 1980 elder abuse received further attention, with a joint hearing of the Senate and House of Representatives Select Committee on Aging (US House of Representatives 1980; Filinson and Ingman 1989). The Committee heard research findings and the results of the Committee's investigation produced the report *Elder Abuse: An Examination of a Hidden Problem* (US House of Representatives 1981). This early ground work, spearheaded by the Chair of the House Select Committee, Representative Claude Pepper, undoubtedly placed elder abuse on the policy map. Supported by a few other Congress colleagues, a decade-long campaign developed to enact a national elder abuse law patterned after the Child Abuse Prevention Act. According to Filinson and Ingman (1989: 130) such initiatives drew support from 'case studies available at the time that indicated abused elderly persons, like children, were typically dependent upon others for their daily personal care and support'.

The time taken to achieve a national profile can be attributed to both ideological and fiscal expediency. Conservatives, in government throughout this period, argued that problems such as family violence, including child abuse, domestic violence and elder abuse, were better addressed locally. A difficult economic climate and a resultant policy of reductions in welfare spending added to federal reluctance to commit expenditure. It became apparent, by 1989, that not enough votes could be found to ratify national elder abuse legislation. Congressional advocates then changed their approach and added an amendment to the Older Americans Act to provide a small budget to the states for elder abuse prevention. As a result, according to Rosalie Wolf (1994: 12), 'A national elder abuse policy does now exist in the United States, but defers to the states in matters of service delivery'.

Elder abuse has acquired a more conspicuous position under a new title: vulnerable elder rights protection. To secure federal funding, states are required to develop programmes for preventing and treating elder abuse, neglect and exploitation, which must include:

1 public education and outreach;
2 coordination of services;
3 a data information management system;
4 training for individuals, professionals and paraprofessionals;
5 technical assistance that would promote the development of an elder abuse system.

This 1992 legislation also assisted the development of a national centre for elder abuse prevention, funded for four years with a third of a million dollars. The centre is charged with:

1 developing and maintaining a clearing-house on programmes;
2 compiling, publishing and disseminating training materials.

State reporting laws

As of 1988, all states in the US have some form of adult abuse and protection laws. Certain states differentiate by age, whilst others have legislation pertaining to anyone from 18 years upwards. They are thus responsible for investigating suspected cases of elder abuse. The states often devolve this role to other service providers, including contractual working with a range of organizations: social services, health, human resources ombudsman and public welfare law enforcement.

Thobaben (1989: 138) observes that adult abuse and protection laws are based on the US legal precedent that society (represented by the state) 'has the authority to act in a parental capacity for persons who are unable to care for and protect themselves, and thus prevent them from suffering abuse, neglect, or exploitation by those responsible for their care or from self-abuse'. Thobaben (1989) has recommended that a model reporting statute should include the following elements:

1 persons covered – persons 18 and older who lack the functional ability to care for and protect themselves should be covered;
2 reportable behaviour – clear definitions of abuse, neglect, and exploitation should be used;
3 mandatory reporting – reporting should be mandatory for all health and social service professionals who have reasonable cause to suspect or believe an incapacitated individual is a victim of abuse, neglect, or exploitation;
4 failure to report – if a professional fails to report, he or she may be charged with a misdemeanour and be reported to his or her professional licensing agency;

5 immunity – all reporters should be immune from civil and criminal liability if the report is made in good faith and without malice;
6 time of report – the verbal report should be taken immediately and be accompanied by a standardized written report within a specified period;
7 agency to receive report – a single state agency should be designated to receive and investigate reports, and to maintain a central register;
8 initial investigation – the investigation for verification and assessment of abuse should be completed within a prescribed period of time.

Many of these points can now be seen in procedures adopted by other countries. However, a distinguishing factor, when compared with the British and Australian approaches, is the statutory force given to professional action. This emphasis within the US has led to criticism that it serves to criminalize mistreatment, promoting the search for a clear perpetrator and victim (Faulkner 1982; Crystal 1986; Formby 1992). Mandatory reporting, for example, is aimed at abuse, neglect and exploitation, and it is arguable whether the legal procedures that follow from it reflect the most appropriate response, given the numbers involved. National statistics for 1991 (cited in Wolf 1993) indicated that 51 per cent of cases concerned self-neglect, which raises questions over the civil rights and choice available to elders if professionals are mandated to act on what they judge to be an inappropriate lifestyle for an older person. Once self-neglect is omitted from the statistics, neglect accounted for 45 per cent of reported cases, followed by physical abuse at 19 per cent, financial abuse at 17 per cent, and emotional abuse at 14 per cent.

The large percentage of cases consisting of neglect sits uneasily with an approach based on legal measures. As Crystal (1986) and Formby (1992) have pointed out, there is no legal obligation on relatives or other citizens to care for another adult. Formby (1992) cites Alabama's statutory definition of an informal carer as an individual who has the responsibility for the care of the elderly or handicapped person as a result of family relationship as a case in point. Whilst it might be thought that a family member is under some obligation to care (see Chapter 5), it is doubtful whether criminal prosecution on this basis could withstand a legal challenge. Similar legal difficulties arise in those states (California, Connecticut, Idaho, Rhode Island, Washington and Wyoming) that declare 'abandonment' to be a form of abuse (Filinson and Ingman 1989). Abandonment may be interpreted as a statement concerning motivation to care, particularly when placed within a right-wing discourse on the need to reinforce family values. It is not, however, in breach of a strictly legal requirement.

The abuse of elders' civil rights, noted earlier, is, however, in breach of constitutional assurances concerning privacy and self-determination. Mandatory reporting also compromises the confidentiality relied upon in relationships between patients and physicians. Formby (1992) indicates that these civil rights problems are compounded by an assumption, tacit within state legislature on adult protective service but by no means proven, that professionals who report are familiar with and educated about elder abuse. It would seem inappropriate to demand a rigid reporting system if it is based on inadequate knowledge and diagnosis of elder abuse and neglect. This, plus a conflict with professional ethical considerations, may help to explain why in one state with mandatory requirements, only two per cent of reports originated from medical staff (Alliance Elder Abuse Project 1983). Studies in Michigan and North Carolina, both states with mandatory reporting, found that 71 per cent of physicians did not know that reporting was a duty and 12 per cent actually thought it was not mandatory at all (O'Brien 1985). Unfortunately, there is little evidence to suggest that this state of affairs has improved since these early studies took place. For example, a special edition of the *Annals of Emergency Medicine* (Sanders 1992) indicates that: 'most emergency departments do not have protocols for detecting and dealing with elder abuse . . . 27% only reporting a protocol'.

Lessons from the US experience

As will be apparent from the above review, the US experience has been mixed in terms of lessons for other countries. This is most clearly shown in terms of the role of state legislature. On the one hand, helping professionals have been given a clear mandate under which to pursue elder protective practice, the absence of which can lead to inactivity and confusion. On the other, the nature of adult protection services, in particular where mandatory reporting has been adopted, may lead to criminalization of what can be a complex interpersonal situation (see Chapter 5). Some resistance can also be detected where professional ethics or notions of civil rights conflict with local statutes. A historical reliance on state legislature has also led to national fragmentation concerning the definition of abuse and neglect and action that can be taken. As much of the ground-breaking research in this field has been conducted under these conditions, the difficulty in obtaining standard definitions, as outlined in Chapter 3, is perhaps understandable. The relatively recent setting up of a national centre should do much to reduce difficulties in this area.

Whilst the exceptional power of lobbying and pressure group systems is perhaps unique to the US context, the role of the media in raising the profile of mistreatment and the finding of a political sponsor in Claude Pepper have done much to influence social policy. By comparison, in the UK very few parliamentary questions have been asked about elder abuse (*Hansard* 1982) and the issue has not emerged on the political agenda.

Research money in the US has continued to flow, and sustained pressure from findings and the National Committee on Elder Abuse has done much to influence revisions to initial and perhaps over-hasty initiatives.

In terms of lessons, then, the role of national coordination, when practice initiatives have been left to local administration, could be transferred to other Western nations. The twin trends of right-wing concern about the growth of welfare spending and attempts to off-load responsibility on to local initiative have ensured that the problem of fragmentation is widespread and needs to be addressed. A national grouping that serves to keep the issue alive as political interest waxes and wanes would also be a valuable addition in most Western contexts. The UK body Action on Elder Abuse is an example of trying to capitalize on US success in this area. Perhaps a final lesson can be drawn from difficulties encountered at later stages if policy initiatives are not grounded in adequate research. This problem may have repeated itself in the UK, an argument which will be elaborated in Chapter 6.

European initiatives

European acknowledgement that elder abuse exists has been slow to mature (Decalmer and Glendenning 1993). In 1990 a study group on violence against elderly people reported work in 22 countries (Council of Europe 1992). Much of this work can be considered as formative, outlining where reference is made, or more accurately can be intrepreted as being made, to elder abuse, in national and regional documents. In many ways progress is at a similar point to early consciousness-raising work in the UK (Baker 1975; Eastman 1983). Scandinavian countries appear to be progressing more quickly with a policy response. In Norway, a pilot project funded by the Ministry of Social Affairs is in progress. This project has built on the work of a number of researchers (Hydle and Johns 1992; Johns *et al.* 1992; Hydle 1994). Norway is perhaps unique in initiating an 'Elder Protective Services' project. The project succeeds in specifying services which have elder protection as their primary concern whilst using established methods of intervention. Johns and Juklestad (1994) comment that: 'information, training, guidance and having a key-person appointed . . . these are, basically, wellknown methods of social work. What we have done is to find a way to implement them in a new field, that of elder abuse.' An original pilot service has been expanded to include a regional network of specialist centres.

Australian initiatives

The Australian response has focused on the states, each of which has developed strategies for intervention. Variations in response therefore reflect local existing service provision. In 1993, the Commonwealth established the Working Party on Protection of Frail Older People in the Community. This working party is designed to supplement the work in progress to protect the rights of residents in nursing homes. The emerging view suggests that elder abuse should be considered as a manifestation of family breakdown and domestic violence (Commonwealth Office for the Aged 1993). It therefore follows that existing community health and welfare resource agencies should be the mainstay of social policy intervention allied to existing legislation on the inspection of residential homes. In defence of this stance the Commonwealth Office for the Aged (1993: 25) states: 'alerting these agencies to the need for protection of frail older people . . . is seen to be a preferred option rather than establishing a separate elder protection service'.

The American concept of mandatory reporting legislation has also been rejected by most states.

State approaches

There are various state initiatives. New South Wales has for example focused on research and education, drawing on the seminal work of Kurrle *et al.* (1991, 1992). Victoria has established a task force in order to promote the formation of networks of local and regional agencies within existing service provision. It has been argued that specialized protection services will not be required when this supportive network is functional. South Australia has established an elder protection programme, which has been funded for staff and training. This programme complements existing service provision and addresses intake, assessment and intervention. South Australia has declined to move towards mandatory reporting laws. Finally, Western Australia has focused on protocol production and dissemination of information about elder abuse to seniors and members of the general public.

The British response to elder abuse

British awareness of elder abuse as a social problem has been long in gestation (see Chapter 1). Initial interest in 'granny battering' (Baker 1975; Burston 1977; Eastman 1983) failed to provoke any policy response. Perhaps the most important event at this time was a conference called by the British Geriatrics Society, a predominantly medical body, in 1989. This event served to draw together professionals who had been working independently but had not previously known each other. However, it had little effect either on physicians as a whole or on other professional groups, leaving progress to be made by a small number of committed individuals.

In 1991, the Social Services Inspectorate, part of the Department of Health, published a study of two London boroughs in order to obtain some idea of the incidence of the problem. Whilst 64 cases had been identified, responding was piecemeal, and lacked coordination and a proper understanding of appropriate procedures for intervention. Government responses to the survey gave an ambivalent message to helping agencies, with the Minister of State, Virginia Bottomley, being widely reported in the professional press as claiming that elder abuse was not a significant problem.

The year 1993 became something of a watershed in terms of British recognition of elder mistreatment. From May till July, *Community Care*, the trade journal for social work in the UK, ran a high-profile campaign drawing attention to the problem. In July, the Department of Health published its own guidelines entitled *No Longer Afraid: The Safeguard of Older People in Domestic Settings* (see Chapter 5). This publication was significant in social policy terms insofar as it was endorsed by the new minister for social services, John Bowis, and gave the green light for local authorities to develop their own policies and procedures. Age Concern England, a leading charity for older people, simultaneously hosted a new pressure group entitled 'Action on Elder Abuse' in order to maintain the profile of the problem amongst concerned pro-fessionals. It was hoped that such an approach would mirror the successes of the National Committee for the Prevention of Elder Abuse in the US.

The emergence of elder mistreatment as a social policy issue in the UK thus exhibits certain characteristics. There was, for example, no attempt to identify specific elder protection legislation, as has been the case in some other countries. *No Longer Afraid* refers to existing general and protective legislation, supplemented by legislation framed to deal with domestic violence and the law of tort. Provision was seen as occurring under the broad umbrella of the 1990

NHS and Community Care Act, which was not perceived as needing modification.

This is in stark contrast to the emergence of child abuse as a social problem. There, a number of high-profile cases achieved broad media attention accompanied by general public outcry and raised consciousness about the issue. Two such cases, that of Jasmine Beckford and the uncovering of child sexual abuse in Cleveland, had a direct influence on the 1989 Children Act. This Act constituted a concerted attempt to systematize existing legislation into a coherent body based on contemporary research into child care. Whereas the 1989 Act drew heavily on these experiences and provided a much-needed clarification of values and procedure, the same cannot be said of the 1990 Act. The latter is generally understood to be an attempt at social engineering of the welfare economy (Phillipson 1990; Biggs 1990a; Means and Smith 1994). It gave little detail to practitioners, this being left to a number of instruments and guidance papers.

Using Blumer's (1971) model of developmental stages for social problems (emergence, legitimation, mobilization, official action and implementation), it could be argued that elder abuse has failed to engage certain key processes as it emerged in the UK. As Blumer (1971: 305) predicts that 'Social problems have their being, career and their fate in this process', such failure may have lasting effects on the development of responses to elder mistreatment. It is worth looking in more detail at the process of problem formation and its influence on policy implementation.

First, there has been little public outcry or grass-roots organization around the issue. This is particularly marked when compared not only with child abuse but also with the related problem of domestic violence. It is therefore unclear how far initiatives on elder mistreatment will both reflect and be sustained by pressure from below, most notably the victims themselves and older people in general.

Second, concern has almost entirely been professional in nature, and then only amongst small groups of practitioners. Question marks remain, therefore, as to how far policy initiatives will be driven by sectional interests as preventive practice develops. Whilst research and practice initiatives have not received significant state funding, as they have in the US context, the influence of government approval on the view taken on mistreatment by such unstable and under-resourced groupings should not be underestimated.

Third, official action has been ambivalent in nature, drawing on existing legislation designed for other purposes and with no additional funding to stimulate a concerted response. Whilst research has been sparse on UK prevalence and incidence, a single study has perhaps played an uncharacteristically significant role in raising policymakers' awareness that something had to be done. Ogg and Bennet's (1992) study, using national survey data, provided evidence that could not be so easily ignored by government ministers and contributed to a policy reversal that contributed to lending elder mistreatment social problem status. An essentially pragmatic political response, based on so little evidence, has not helped to resolve tensions over continuing controversy, such as the adequacy of the 1990 NHS and Community Care Act as a vehicle for elder protection work.

Finally, and as a result of the above, implementation has been piecemeal. Most of the planning was left to local authorities, and lacked central coordination. Certain social services departments (most notably Cambridgeshire, Tower Hamlets, Norfolk and Wallsall) approached this new responsibility with remarkable determination. However, a key policy issue concerns the degree to which official sanction is given to inter-agency collaboration. This has been an important factor driving responses to child protection (Hallet and Birchall 1992). Where collaboration between health, social services and law enforcement on elder mistreatment has emerged, it has done so because of existing good relations. Those areas where this has not already been the case are given no policy impetus to achieve it, although these might be precisely the areas where corrective action is most needed.

Partly as a consequence of this history, the 'claims making activity' that Gusfield (1984) and Best (1989) identify as part and parcel of the construction of social problems seems to have gone into reverse. 'Claimsmakers' are groups who are active in drawing attention to a problem. For Best (1989) this process usually draws to a close once a policy to deal with the problem has been devised by officials. In the British case, guidance to social services, the closest yet to formal recognition of the problem by government, seems to have prompted the initiation of pressure group activity, rather than being part of claims-maker achievement.

The dangers in such a history are that policy statements are based neither on political will in response to grass-roots agitation, nor on a considered overview of research into the problem and associated professional interventions. The birth of elder abuse as a recognized social problem, has, instead, reflected a number of contradictions within existing social policy, plus an unholy brew of common-sense assumptions about the problem that are not borne out by US research (see Chapters 3 and 5).

Explaining the nature of the emergence of elder mistreatment in UK settings

A number of writers have attempted to explain why elder mistreatment has emerged in this way in the UK. Kingston and Penhale (1995: 229–30), propose that the status obtained by elder abuse in social problem terms is related to the view taken of older people in society in general:

> Elderly people are increasingly viewed as dependent and a burden on the rest of society by virtue of their age. . . . That elder abuse exists may indeed be related to such negative stereotypes of old age. . . . Currently held ideologies about old age and ageing may create environments which encourage the development and perpetuation of abusive situations.

Kingston and Penhale (1995: 230) go on to argue that the way that mistreatment is conceived as a social policy issue reflects these deep-seated prejudices about the nature of the ageing process. This may help to explain why elder abuse 'does not yet appear to have achieved the full status of a social problem'.

These authors also amplify concern, noted by Manthorpe (1993), that if the social construction of elder mistreatment remains an exclusively professional domain, it will become part of the 'ageing enterprise'. This term was first coined by Estes (1979) to satirize the deliberate attempt to construct a problem by vested interests in the US, who then establish services and professional careers without reference to the expressed needs of older people themselves. The 'discovery' of elder mistreatment would then contribute to the further marginalization of older people within society.

Phillipson (1993, 1994; Phillipson and Biggs 1995) notes that the history of elder abuse has to be seen both as a reflection of a political economy that systematically excludes older people from economic and social rights, and as part of the growth of knowledge of ageing processes in the health and welfare sphere (see also Chapter 2).

Elder abuse may not have become a social policy issue until recently for a number of inter-related reasons.

First, the dominance of welfare paternalism following the birth of the welfare state meant that it was extremely difficult to question the integrity of the family as the basic unit of caring in society. However, by the 1970s, a growing awareness of child abuse and domestic violence severely dented the image of the family as a haven in a harsh world. Both of these issues developed champions, through either existing charitable concerns or the growth of the feminist movement, which leant ideological strength to the need for change and significant grass-roots activity.

Second, increased use of health and welfare services by a growing elderly population both raised professional awareness of issues related to ageing and increased policymakers' concern that this 'non-productive' part of the population would become a 'burden' on the public purse, with little or no benefit to society. Social policy was thus influenced by the development of a distinctive body of knowledge, termed gerontology, and by fiscal concerns regarding older age in ways that had not previously been the case. The time-lag between this growing awareness and that of other policy areas, such as family violence in its other forms, helps to explain why the mistreatment of specifically elderly citizens did not develop a higher profile sooner. Indeed, awareness of domestic violence and child abuse paved the way for the recognition of elder abuse, creating a climate in which it could be identified. Whilst this process has helped the visibility of elder mistreatment, it has also contributed to it being seen through the lens of similar, but distinctive, social problems, rather than developing responses arising from the unique position of older people.

Third, the 1980s and early 1990s saw a new moral agenda which challenged the idea of dependency on the state. A key development, arising from fiscal concern, was an increased emphasis on the role of the family and friends as primary carers. Families were seen as being under an obligation to care for their older members, thus reducing reliance on formal services. Care for older people within families thus came into a sharper, but different, focus from that characteristic of the agendas already outlined above. The ability of significant others to look after older people became a central plank of policy as envisaged in the 1990 NHS and Community Care Act. Factors that cast doubt on this role were not welcomed by policymakers during that period.

Biggs (1993a, 1994) has drawn attention to the parallel timing of the implementation of the 1990 Act and the growth in professional concern about elder mistreatment. He proposes that a combination of continued ageism in social policy plus the new right's ideological concern with individualism resulted in the emergence of 'failed individuals', who are not only dependent on others but are seen as morally deficient in being so (see Chapter 2).

Such people cannot participate in the right-wing project of individualism because they have, of necessity, to negotiate their needs with other people for continued material and social existence. They can, however, become a repository for the psychological dependency of others. As dependency is associated with weakness and other unwanted aspects of the personality, rejection, and even punishment, are implicitly sanctioned.

The 1990 Act, by emphasizing the role of informal care, supported by professionals whose job it was to coordinate 'care packages' around this basic unit, effectively eclipsed the dominance of older people's needs. These became replaced by the ability of the carer to function in what was effectively a paraprofessional role. Professional helpers and informal carers were now conceived, in policy terms, as having a similar relationship to the nominated dependent. This would increase task-related empathy between the two, raising the danger of collusion that further marginalized the victim (see Chapter 5).

However, during the 1990s, both the narcissistic longings of individualism and community care policy began to encounter practical difficulties. Concerned practitioners and critics of the government's approach found, in elder maltreatment,confirmation of many of their reservations about the new right's reforms. Elder mistreatment paradoxically (Biggs 1994) became a vehicle by which an older person's civil and human rights could be placed on the policy agenda, without the stigma associated with an exclusive emphasis on dependency.

These attempts to explain the history of elder abuse as a social problem have different starting points. They converge on the need to see the phenomenon within the broader framework of the position of elders in British society and the way that policy can shape the positioning of practical responses to the exclusion of other options.

Conclusions

Whilst developments in different countries have taken different routes, it is possible to sketch preliminary recommendations on the direction of future social policy. First, political ambivalence and a devolution to local initiatives can lead to uneven and truncated development of services. Where this has been the case, some form of national coordination will be needed to work towards standardization of what can be defined as mistreatment and the monitoring and dissemination of service innovations.

Second, the effective containment of the problem to considerations of domestic abuse would need to be challenged if a more comprehensive picture is to emerge. Institutional abuse and neglect is the most salient area in which a uniform awareness and procedure is called for. Otherwise elders could simply be transferred from one abusive situation to another.

Third, policy makers should be alert to the danger of professional interest groups producing an 'ageing enterprise', whereby the voice of elders and carers are effectively eclipsed. Hearing these voices may result in maltreatment being placed in the wider social and economic circumstances of these groups. Whilst this message may be difficult for politicians to digest, it is essential if responses to the phenomenon are to be grounded in the daily experience of abuse and for policy to make a comprehensive response to the requirements identified.

Fourth, the road to criminalization has led to the identification of a number of problems. These include conflict over the legal grounds for taking action, polarization of a complex interpersonal problem, leading to an adversarial stance which may detract from long-term solutions being found, and reluctance by professionals to engage in reporting. It is instructive that few countries have followed the US lead in this area.

Finally, whilst debate continues over the promotion of adult protection, as opposed to specific emphasis on elder mistreatment, it is clear that policy should extend to wider considerations of older people in society and their use of health, criminal justice and welfare services. Policy initiatives should make specific reference to inter-agency collaboration as a cornerstone of service provision. If guidance is directed at only one agency, the problem of coordination at a later stage will be amplified.

5

Family and community

Introduction

This chapter examines the social construction of family and community, with special reference to the nature of public and private space. These factors, it is argued, have led to the perception of elder mistreatment as being located in particular settings, most notably the family, to the exclusion of other contexts. The state has played a significant role in reinforcing this trend and guidance from the British Department of Health is critically assessed. Attention is paid to debates over the role of family obligations to care, situational stress and dependency, plus notions of cultures of violence and role reversal across the life course. Unfortunately, these debates have paid little attention to carer coping strategies, the possibility of collusion between carers and professional helpers in community settings, the visibility of abuse in the community and the growing problem of community harassment. These factors are discussed in turn and conclusions drawn for future practice.

Ageing in contemporary society

In industrial societies, following a predominantly Western blueprint, certain forms of relations are judged to be normative, and certain perspectives more valid. A tension that arises within systems in which the possibilities for choice are ambiguous concerns the degree to which social actors behave in conformity with roles that are socially created and maintained. Both family and community will place expectations on members concerning, for example, the care of relatives, degree of engagement in social life, and other priorities which affect perceptions of self and others. This can be demonstrated through a brief examination of the social construction of ageing.

Butler (1963, 1987: 22) was amongst the first to characterize attitudes towards older age as ageism, which he conceived as: 'A process of systematic stereotyping and discrimination against people because they are old, just as racism and sexism accomplish this for skin colour and gender'. Ageism, he claims, allows younger people to see elders as different from themselves. They cease to identify with elders as human beings and thereby reduce their own fears of ageing. It also becomes a useful expedient whereby decision takers in society can promote viewpoints about older people in order to relieve themselves of responsibility towards them.

Social expectation often requires that ageing be seen as a handicap which disqualifies the actor from certain activities. Social interaction may be structured in a way that reinforces the negative consequences of ageing (Giles and Coupland 1991). Indeed, the presence of older people may serve as an unwelcome reminder to younger adults of what the future may hold and thus provoke personal avoidance and marginalization (Biggs 1989b; Bytheway 1994). The common-sense assumptions held by other adults allow elders to be treated as if difficulties in one area of functioning can be generalized to everything the older person does. Reasons for approaching health and welfare agencies, such as disability or economic hardship, might be taken, for example, to imply that the older person cannot make decisions for him- or herself. Older adults may choose to respond to this ascribed role in a number of ways. They may conform to the expectations of others on whom they depend for certain services, reject the culture of the younger adult and seek out the society of people with similar social disadvantages, or challenge age-ascribed common sense through either individual or collective action.

It follows from this analysis that older people may experience specific problems when engaging with health and welfare systems, by virtue of attitudes towards ageing that are common in our wider society (Kuhn 1977). These may take a particular form when attempts to meet older people's requirements need to negotiate boundaries between organizations, community and family.

Public and private space in community settings

The social construction of family and community and the relation between the two create a social space that is both external and limiting to members whilst allowing a degree of self-directed action. One of the distinctions made between family and community in British society rests on conceptions of public and private space. Family relations exist in what has been conceived of as a private sphere. That is to say, boundaries around the family, and most notably the family home, are relatively impermeable and protective of members. Outsiders enter only on the assumption of restraint and respect for established norms of behaviour. They may have expectations about the behaviour that should be found within family boundaries, but rarely have permission to comment on or attempt to change it (Froggatt 1990; Hargrave and Anderson 1992).

Whilst norms exist for maintaining personal boundaries in community settings, it is an essentially visible, public space. Boundaries are relatively permeable and a common code of expected behaviour is generally understood. This gives rise to common-sense assumptions that are taken as given by social actors in that sphere (Goffman 1963). It may only be when people encounter different communities with different cultures and social norms that they become aware of the arbitrary nature of their own assumptions (Cicourel 1973).

That family and community are differently located with respect to public and private spheres becomes problematic once behaviour held to be deviant in the public sphere, such as mistreatment, emerges from the private sphere and becomes visible to a wider audience (Biggs 1993a). This is especially the case if there are statutory responsibilities on those who have to cross from the public to the private. This is the position that many professional helpers find themselves in and can lead to conflict over the balance between confidentiality and statutory obligation, respect for individual family culture and wider social norms, and attention to collusive arrangements which might result.

Both of these factors, socially constructed attitudes to older age and attitudes to public and private domains, will contribute to the way that behaviour is located and responded to.

Locating family, community and mistreatment

The relationship between community, family and mistreatment has been subject to definition and redefinition. Biggs (1993a) has noted how these boundaries have changed, depending upon the political perspectives of different interests. Commentators on the left have emphasized the caring potential of networks and collective identity in daily life (Hadley 1982; Leonard 1984; Bornat *et al.* 1985). Boundaries between the personal and public spheres are seen as permeable, once the benefits of mutual support are encouraged and experienced. A virtuous circle of increasing interdependency would make the community a safer environment and the family less defended against external threat and less likely to be forced into a position where the family exclusively contains stress to the detriment of the quality of life of those within it.

Right-wing social policy has focused on freeing individuals from the dependency of others whilst simultaneously underscoring family responsibility (Thompson 1989). It is concerned both with removing constraints to individual enterprise in the public sphere, and with ensuring that obligations in the private sphere are undertaken. Expectations of behaviour in the two spheres are thus quite different and rely on the maintenance of rigid boundaries between the public and private. Commentators in North America (Minkler and Robertson 1991) and in Britain (Thompson 1989; Phillipson 1991) have observed that this approach is in part driven by fears that the 'welfare contract' between generations has broken down. Younger people, it is argued, can no longer be relied upon to care for those who are not economically productive members of society. This concern has been translated into attempts to ensure that family obligation is reinforced and that 'responsibility is placed as near to the individual and his carer as possible' (Griffiths 1988: 3).

Feminist approaches differ in emphasis between debates in the US on women as victims of violence (Yllo 1993; Kurz 1993) and those in the UK on the effects of carer burden. A number of UK feminist writers (Finch 1984; Dalley 1988) have pointed out that care by the community is in practice reducible to care within the family by female carers. It thus strengthens and perpetuates women's dependency within the family. According to Finch (1988: 5): 'Propounders of the familial ideal favour it because for them it embodies notions of the family as haven, as responsibility and affection and thus a private protection against a cold,hostile outside world'.

The feminist viewpoint tends to emphasize the need to liberate carers from the restrictions of roles that define women in terms of the services they provide to others (Hamner and Statham 1988). Morris (1992) has questioned this perspective, noting that it tends to ally feminism exclusively with the needs of oppressed carers and does not address the requirements of those who are cared for. Morris (1992: 32) argues:

> Insult is then added to injury by the assumption that for a disabled person to aspire to warm, caring human relationships within the setting where most non-disabled people look to find such relationships is a form of false consciousness. We are to be denied not only the rights non-disabled people take for granted, but when we demand these rights we are told we are wrong to do so.

She proposes that 'caring about' has somehow become lost in the debate around 'caring for'. It is almost taken as a given that the caring enterprise is not a reciprocal process and that in many cases the essential interdependence of relationships, and thus their strength, is eclipsed. An exclusively feminist approach would also ignore significant numbers of male carers. For example, the most vulnerable group of carers, spouses aged over 75, contains more men than women, in a ratio 5 to 3 (Parker 1990).

Formal community care arrangements have also been criticized as Euro-centric (Patel 1990, 1994; Mizra 1991). It is pointed out that community consists of many different cultural experiences. However, the dominant culture rarely takes account of the differing needs, under-use of traditional services and pre-existing supportive and defensive networks operating amongst minority ethnic groups. It is often assumed that these groups are self-contained and, at least in the family sphere, 'take care of themselves', reinforcing boundaries both between cultures and between the public and the private. This is in spite of observations that, in the case of mistreatment (George 1994: 163), 'Ethnic elderly people are likely to be at increased risk because of a combination of multiple risk factors not present in the indigenous population'.

The growth of interest in elder mistreatment also needs to be set against the way that older people and the difficulties they face are presented to the wider society. A number of authors (Mullen and Von Zwanenberg 1988; Nussbaum *et al.* 1989; Rodwell *et al.* 1992) have noted that media coverage of elders is skewed towards frailty and vulnerability. Further, the structure of media reporting favours single events, catastrophes or scandals over enduring problems. Elder abuse is newsworthy in ways that problems such as poverty, social isolation and the negotiation of appropriate support are not. There is a danger (Phillipson 1993; Biggs and Phillipson 1994) that the high profile given to abusive situations might override other problems encountered by elders and the resources allocated to them. Abuse may come to eclipse other problems that older people and their support networks encounter.

Each of the above perspectives would locate elder mistreatment differently as a social problem. Left-wing commentators would see abuse as a consequence of the isolation enforced on families, external sources of stress and the erosion of community networks. A right-wing analysis would emphasize the erosion of obligation within families and the failure of services to offer adequate choice in supportive arrangements to maintain familial duty. An inter-ethnic perspective might draw attention to the inappropriateness of service delivery systems and the dangers of cultural stereotyping. Whatever the motivation behind community care, the rights of carers and the nominated cared-for are differentially emphasized by feminists and the disability movement. Both would place abuse within the context of social stereotypes and an imbalance of power within relationships.

Formal location of elder mistreatment

An example of the systematic positioning of elder mistreatment can be found in Department of Health (1993) guidelines, *No Longer Afraid: The Safeguard of Older People in Domestic Settings*. As the title suggests, the phenomenon has been located in a certain social space, namely a family environment or failing that within the victim's own home. It obscures the possibility of recognizing mistreatment in others, for example in forms of community harassment or in institutional care.

Within that setting, according to the Department of Health (1993: 4):

There are likely to be many different reasons why older people are abused. Carers under stress, or ill equipped for the caring role, and carers who have been (and are still being) abused themselves, account for a proportion of cases. A history of poor family relationships is a reason for others. In some families, the power once exercised by the parent becomes transferred to the son or daughter and this change of balance is also probably a factor.

This conception of mistreatment leads to certain factors being seen as causal and thus implies a particular history for abusive relationships. For example, an emphasis on carer stress and suitability would indicate that difficulty associated with the caring role itself generates grounds for mistreatment. The likelihood of abuse and neglect would depend upon how relationships within the family have developed over time. More precisely, role reversals between parents and children may play a decisive factor.

The location of mistreatment is thus tacitly refined to focus on the frustrations of filial obligation in which family history repeats itself with intergenerational roles reversed. Spouse abuse, the role of external pressure upon the family unit, and the absence of reparative services are not given prominence.

It is suggested by the Department of Health (1993: 1) that 'Any framework for intervention should be considered in relation to . . . care management and assessment'. Care management has become a central component of community care. It evolved in the US as a means of coordinating a fragmented service system, often determined by incomplete insurance cover (Moxley 1989; Austin and O'Connor 1989). In the UK context, care management has been used to coordinate packages of services in a mixed welfare economy, usually in order to support the informal care of nominated clients/patients and thus maintain them in their domestic setting (Challis and Davies 1986; Griffiths 1988; HMSO 1990).

Two examples of care packages are given in *No Longer Afraid*. These refer to 'different types of service for different situations'. The first refers to carer stress and includes information, day or respite care, nursing support and carer support schemes. The second concerns 'abusive environments' and includes advocacy, refuges, legal intervention, counselling or removal of the carer, institutional care or rehousing. However, the Department of Health (1993: 15) notes: 'In the main, agencies should be providing packages of care which, subject to the views of users, enable people to remain in their own homes'.

Considerable stress is laid on the value of systematic monitoring and review, although the precise nature and function of this process is not made clear. Under 'Access to assistance', it is noted by the Department of Health (1993: 11) that: 'However much information is provided, some may not wish to avail themselves of it, because of pride, a sense of duty or feeling that their problem is a family matter, not for sharing with others'.

Elder mistreatment is therefore firmly located within the domestic environment. It is predominantly seen as an intergenerational problem arising either from stress in the immediate caring situation or as a consequence of long-term family relationships. Suggested intervention varies, depending upon these circumstances, and would either focus upon support to the carer in order to reduce stress or removal of the older person from an abusive environment. Whilst difficulties in negotiating professional entry to the private sphere are recognized, no systematic guidance is offered. One option might be to continue to monitor the situation. Another, implied by the inclusion of a substantial appendix on the legal grounds for intervention, would be to move from a frame of reference based on consent to one based on coercion.

Given the persistence of beliefs about family obligation, carer stress and the intergenerational transmission of violence, it is worth examining each in some detail.

Family obligation and exchange

Obligation to care within families has been subject to study during the period leading up to the UK reform of community care, with conclusions different to the concerns of policy makers. According to Janet Finch (1989: 242):

In reality, the 'sense of obligation' which marks the distinctive character of kin relationships is nothing like its image in the political debate where it appears as a set of ready-made moral rules which all right-thinking people accept and put into practice.

Whilst there seem to be implicit rules and expectations about reciprocal care, these are negotiated within the private space of each family and the particular circumstances of family members (Phillipson 1992, 1994). A formal focus on care by family members may owe more to other policy concerns, such as concern about the cost of residential care to the public purse (Biggs 1991), and may attempt to move the balance of services away from universal social rights and towards targeted and therefore contingent benefits (Salter 1994). Studies on elders' expectations of formal services (West *et al.*1984; Salvage *et al.* 1989) show an unwillingness to place the major burden of care on to other family members. Daughters, for example, should not be expected to give up work opportunities to care for their ageing parents.

It appears from research (George 1986; Finch 1989; Finch and Mason 1990) that intergenerational obligation is largely unidirectional. That is to say, older generations expect to offer support and guidance to younger ones, with little pressure to balance out these gifts. If there are norms for family behaviour, they would seem to be centred on creating optimal circumstances for the family to reproduce itself in succeeding generations.

Rules for relations between second and third generations are far less clear than between the second and the first. They are generally absent from our social repertoire and require re-learning as circumstances change (Minuchin 1974; Schneewind 1990; Biggs 1993a). Families may run into problems because of difficulties in allocating clear responsibilities. Minuchin (1974: 95) suggests that: 'because of the complexity of the family unit, there may be a number of vague boundaries which create confusion and stress'.

Families who have experienced migration (Young and George 1991; George 1994), predominantly from minority ethnic cultures in the UK, may also experience disrupted intergenerational expectations between first, second and third generations. George (1994) surmises that the competing personal and cultural loyalties that can emerge may give rise to conflict, which is stored up and released at times of ill-health.

The unidirectionality of expectation dominant in contemporary Western culture, coupled with few clear guidelines for intergenerational negotiation, becomes particularly acute in times when circumstances are subject to change. 'The transition from carer to cared for might therefore be expected to occasion considerable existential dislocation, both for older people and their carers' (Biggs 1993a: 129).

This is not to say that the middle generation fails to negotiate informal care. Finch and Mason (1990) found that procedural rules existed between children to reduce conflict in working out how caring should take place. These consisted of what could be called a hierarchy of intimacy. Spouses were expected to care before children, who were expected to contribute before other relatives, regardless of the quality of the relationship. Which children provided care depended on the gender of the person receiving care, rather than automatically falling upon the daughter, which might reflect taboos on intimate physical tending. The acceptability of any solution seemed to depend on roles being shared 'equitably but not equally' between those in an equivalent generational position. Cantor (1983) has proposed, citing findings from the US, that a 'principle of centrality' governs caring and identifies the closest relative to the older person as the principal carer. It was also found that female kin were more likely to be assigned or assume this role, reflecting traditional sex-role stereotyping. Successful resolution was not simply a matter for the private sphere, but also held an important role in managing family reputation in the public arena.

Cicirelli (1986) has indicated that it is not so much a sense of obligation that ensured satisfactory caring, but the strength of an underlying bond of affection between elder and carer. Similarly, concrete reward does not seem to play a strong role in continuance of care (Finch and Wallis 1993). George (1986) points out that consideration of what she calls 'equity' (that rewards and resources should flow in both directions even if this be distributed over a lifetime) and 'solidarity', regardless of reward between significant others, will vary depending upon the carer's relationship to the dependent elder. Equity, both between the elder and carer and with other relatives, became more of an issue as expectations to care moved from spousal, through filial, to relationships with in-laws. However, 'Our greatest risk is not that solidarity is somehow losing out to concerns of equity. Rather our greatest risk is that family members will not place limits on solidarity such that their own wellbeing can be sustained' (George 1986: 90).

When caring is based on obligation alone, mistreatment would seem to be made more, not less, likely if, for example, carers perceive their situation as enforced by duty or public embarrassment (Phillips 1986: 203). When both elders and carers perceive themselves as having no choice in continuing the relationship, 'the person with the power advantage develops a monopoly on rewards and has little to lose by being unjust'. According to this exchange theory of abuse, obligation might actually increase the likelihood of mistreatment.

Carer stress and victim dependency

Carer stress is perhaps the most common folk explanation of elder mistreatment, in spite of increasing evidence that immediate situational stress is a marginal factor in actual cases (Pillemer and Wolf 1986; Pillemer 1993).

The relationship between stress and mistreatment has succinctly been described by Bennet and Kingston (1993) in the following way. Increased dependency in the older person leads to stress in the carer which results in abuse and neglect. Phillips (1986) notes that stress is thereby explained through the use of a 'situational model'. There would thus seem to be a direct and easily understood relationship between the frustrations of caring and responses that maltreat those cared for (see Chapter 2).

The tenacity of this common-sense understanding of mistreatment has become something of a puzzle for researchers. Baumann (1989) believes that stress brought elder abuse quickly to the attention of the US public, by drawing analogies from child abuse work, while Pillemer (1993) traces early attempts to link abuse to the 'sudden, unwarranted dependency of parents' on potential carers. Biggs (1994) has noted that situational stress makes elder abuse understandable to younger professionals and policy makers, who might not otherwise be able to identify with issues surrounding the tasks of later life. However, this link fosters identification with the carer at the cost of locating the victim as a 'burden'. In short, the victim becomes the problem.

Whatever the reason for its popularity, empirical evidence has rarely supported the dependency–stress hypothesis. Pillemer (1993) discounts a number of 'stress-related' findings because no comparison was made with non-abusive relationships (see Chapter 3). Further, the three stressors that distinguish abusive and non-abusive situations – someone moving into the household, someone leaving and someone getting arrested (Pillemer and Wolf 1986) – reflect wider social problems than simple dependency.

Steinmetz (1993: 231–2; Steinmetz and Amsden 1983) observed a much stronger relationship 'between subjective feelings of stress and burden as a result of having to assist the elder and abuse of the elder. . . . Caregivers who lived with an elder and had total responsibility for his or her care were more likely to be physically abusive'. She proposes that abuse is less likely if other family members support the carer. Unfortunately, she (wrongly) cites Phillips (1983) in support of this position (see p. 231). Phillips (1983, 1986) actually found that:

> The only category of social support that had a direct relationship to abuse was the number of family members in the household other than the caregiver available to help. The relationship was positive; the *more* people other than the caregiver available to help, the *more* abuse [author's italics].
>
> (1986: 200)

When interpreted correctly, Phillips' findings would imply the possibility of scapegoating and victimization of the older person as much as positive support to the task of caring.

An extensive review of carer burden (Montgomery 1989) indicates that the distinction between objective stressors and the subjective experience of stress is a valid one to make. Many carers live in circumstances of considerable financial hardship, restricted social opportunity and difficult caring tasks, yet do not report excessive stress. Others appear to be easily stressed by minimal changes associated with caring. Montgomery criticizes the assumption that many researchers make, that caring is by its very nature an oppressive and negative experience. She did not, however, extend her review to elder mistreatment.

Wolf (1986: 223) states that 'Provocative behaviour by victims, coupled with unrealistic expectations and financial and medical problems of the per-petrators, seemed to create a more stressful environment for the abused families than that found in the non-abused sample'. Both she and Hudson (1986) point out that it is impossible to say in such cases whether stress occurs before abuse and therefore causes it or is a consequence of abuse having taken place. Wolf (1989) later distinguished, in a report to the US House of Representatives, between different forms of mistreatment and their causes. Victims of physical and psychological abuse tended to have emotional problems, but be otherwise physically well. Abusers had a history of mental illness or substance abuse, lived with and were financially dependent on the victim. Victims of neglect had little social support, were very old and both physically and mentally impaired. It was here that carers found their elder a great source of stress. Finally, victims of material abuse were likely to be single, with limited social contacts. Abusers had financial problems, often related to alcohol or drug abuse.

Thus, whilst there is little support for the view that abuse is a direct consequence of situational stress or carer burden, the debate has raised a number of issues suggesting further exploration. First, it would seem that individual differences in how carers and elders construe the caring relationship might significantly affect the likelihood of mistreatment taking place. Second, mistreatment is as much a consequence of carer characteristics as the infirmity of the older person. This would tend to point research in the direction of carer suitability to care and the dynamics of ongoing relationships between perpetrators and victims. Finally, isolation, living arrangements and the association of other social problems, such as alcoholism, drug abuse and financial dependency, suggest that consideration of the way that private and public worlds interact should receive greater attention than they have to date.

Cultures of violence and role reversal in families

Ageist assumptions about the passivity of older people and a focus on the needs of carers can lead to the assumption that mistreatment arises from intergenerational role reversal. That is to say, resentment arising from a turn around in the traditional parent–child relationship in later life as the elder comes to depend upon offspring. This new relationship would go against the norms of intergenerational helping outlined above. It also fits with the folk view of elder abuse (cited by Glendenning 1993), which has been given a number of verse forms:

When I was a Laddie,
I lived with me granny,
And many a hiding me granny g'id me.
Now I am a man,
And I live with my Granny,
And I do unto her what she did unto me.

The moral of this tale is that family violence is transmitted from generation to generation, and there is some evidence for this from the study of child abuse (O'Leary 1993). Similarly, couples with a history of male violence and abuse early in marriage reversed roles once the husband became infirm (Homer and Gilleard 1990). In both cases the debt is repaid once roles are reversed, and violence is a continuing factor in family culture.

A second, but related, view is that reversed roles themselves trigger abuse. Steinmetz (1988, 1993) has proposed that such 'generationally inverse families' are particularly prone to mistreatment. However, this position again suffers from a lack of controlled study.

Role reversal was originally conceived by Rautman (1962) to explain 'neurotic and immature' relations whereby children find themselves 'parenting' their own parents. It has been described by Selzer (1990) as a 'simple, neat concept to reinforce social policy' with little empirical support. She argues that it emphasizes repayment in kind as a required duty, which holds none of the optimism of child-rearing. It thus not only reinforces private obligation, it also casts a shadow of hostility and resentment over the caring enterprise, whilst firmly locating it within the child–parent relationship. This view would not concur with George's (1986) findings on carers' attitudes cited in the preceding section and fails to explain why the majority of carers who are children do not maltreat their parents. It is thus thought to be of limited explanatory value.

A more comprehensive argument has been advanced by Gelles and Straus (1979), linking the family as a social institution to violent relationships.

> The family, with the exception of the military in times of war and the police, is society's most violent institution. The likelihood of being a victim of violence at the hands of a stranger or on the streets is measured in terms of risk per 100,000 people, but the risk of family violence is measured in terms of a rate per 100 individuals.
>
> (Gelles 1993: 35)

Consequently, they propose that tactical conflict (as measured by their Conflict Tactics Scale) is simply an endemic part of negotiating the uniquely intense, intrusive and intimate world of family life. A continuum of physical assault, ranging from shoving and slapping through to murder, exists. The meaning of assault would depend upon the social circumstances in which it takes place. For example, Straus (1993) has argued that assaults by women are less likely to be construed as mistreatment than similar actions by men. Family behaviour is thus predicated on certain accepted levels of conflictual activity both within each private sphere and by society at large. If this argument is extended to elder mistreatment, a tension emerges between what might be acceptable within any one family culture and the public view of acceptable levels of conflict, seen through the perspective of the helping professional (with, it might be added, her or his own history of acceptable family tactics). Whilst this perspective has been extensively applied to domestic abuse between couples, it has not been applied to the area of elder abuse. It would emphasize the active contribution of older people in negotiating conflict, but, as has been pointed out (Jones and Schechter 1992; Yllo 1993), minimizes the motivating role of power and control on the part of the perpetrator.

O'Leary (1993) has made some interesting observations that suggest a continuum of aggressive behaviour in intimate relationships. He proposes that verbal aggression, perhaps provoked by relationship discord, jealousy and misuse of power, should be distinguished from physical aggression. The latter arises where family culture, past or present, models violence and substance misuse. Severe aggression and murder might result from personality disorder and emotional instability. This would suggest that distinctions should be made between severity or type of mistreatment and distinctive causative factors, and to a degree supports Wolf's (1989) conclusions mentioned above. It should not then be assumed that one form of mistreatment leads to another, nor that different types of abuse necessarily cluster together.

So, role reversal would be an unlikely cause of abuse, except perhaps in extremely disturbed family settings where reversal was one factor in family pathology. There is, however, something to be said in seeing negotiation strategies within families as a significant determinant of mistreatment.

Coping strategies and suitability

Our discussion above would indicate that successful caring, and thus the likelihood of mistreatment taking place, depends less on blanket obligation to care and more upon the suitability and compatibility of carers in caring relationships. Cicirelli (1986: 56) concludes that 'Relationships based on obligation alone are likely to be perfunctory in comparison to the qualitatively richer interactions of affection-based relationships'.

If relations are unduly conflictual, Steinman (1979) found that a number of maladaptive strategies might follow. 'Over-zealous approachers' would persist in caring and conflict; 'active avoiders' would neglect the caring role, hoping that others would step in; 'vacillators' would engage in cycles of approach and avoidance, resulting in much uncertainty and anxiety. Only strategies of 'constructive approachers' could resolve problems as they emerged, by recognizing conflict for what it was and taking steps to improve the situation.

Milne *et al.* (1993) found that whilst carer strain was high for all groups of carers with dementing elders, those who developed an 'active cognitive' strategy fared better than carers who adopted behavioural strategies (keeping busy) or avoidance (drinking or smoking more). Active cognitive strategies included thinking about ways of overcoming problems and seeking social support.

LeNavenec (1994) discovered that families with open styles of managing dementia coped better with what she calls the 'illness career' than families with closed styles. An open style included readiness to share information and feelings within and beyond the immediate family unit as well as accepting support from outsiders. Closed-style families found it more difficult to see continuity in the personality of the elder and were less open to finding hope in the future after the elder's death. They were also more likely to attribute difficult behaviour to an elder's personality, and saw the elder as a block on making a life of their own.

These findings both emphasize the importance of the active construction of meaning and the differential aptitude to the caring role. Following Wolf's (1990) conclusions on differences between types of mistreatment and carer characteristics, plus O'Leary's (1993) on a continuum of violent behaviour and causality, it would make sense to consider suitability to care as a significant factor in responding to elder mistreatment. However, it is unclear how far policy reliance on domestic care allows space for such considerations.

Managing the boundary between public and private space: community care and care management

The preceding sections indicate that negotiating the boundary between public and private space (that is, willingness to accept services, social isolation, the effects of co-terminous social problems) is a significant factor affecting successful intervention in cases of suspected elder mistreatment. The relationship between community care services and domestic arrangements have been interpreted in a particular way following the implementation of the 1990 NHS and Community Care Act.

Care management has a key role in fixing the boundary between these different sources of care and therefore is a central factor in determining negotiation between public and private spheres (Biggs 1993b). Manthorpe (1993) has pointed to the positive role that care management can have in reducing elder mistreatment insofar as multidisciplinary support can be coordinated and continuity maintained across services such as domiciliary and residential care. Care management also allows for ongoing monitoring to take place, in line with explicit objectives, and may thus reduce uncertainty in expectations between formal and informal care (Biggs 1991).

However, the particular model of community support that has emerged from the 1990 Act has been subject to criticism (Phillipson 1990; Biggs 1990a, 1993b; Jack 1992; Biggs and Phillipson 1994). It is felt by these authors that the adoption of an overly administrative model has reduced emphasis on interpersonal processes arising between older service users and professionals, and has increased concern about bureaucratic procedure and financial stewardship within caring agencies.

Factors such as focused contractual specifications and reliance on carers would have specific implications for elder protection. Patel (1994) has expressed concern that purchasing arrangements have often resulted in a forced specialization of community services, particularly amongst black voluntary organizations. She cites the example of an Asian women's group, which was originally set up to deal with domestic violence, being offered funding to provide meals to Asian elders. Not only would this fulfil a different function, it would ensure that the group simply became an extension of existing local authority services. The precarious nature of funding for services to minority groups is a widespread problem, despite their often innovatory nature. The Tower Hamlets Bangladeshi Disability Counselling Service has, for example, provided support to older people amongst others, whose disability was often caused by racial attack. However, its short-term funding means that the service exists under continued uncertainty (Begum and Allen, personal communication, 1994).

Biggs and Phillipson (1994) have argued that placing the carer at the centre of community support can eclipse the perspective of the nominated client, the older person, and reduce the readiness of professional helpers to act on suspicions of mistreatment. This follows from the situation of building formal intervention around support to the carer as the lynchpin of continued maintenance of elders in community settings. If the carer fails in this task, the care package created by the care manager would collapse and, along with it, the policy objective of keeping elders 'in their own homes'.

Reporting and visibility

Penhale (1993) has noted a number of barriers that contribute to a reluctance in reporting mistreatment:

1 the victim may be dependent on the abuser for basic survival and fear retaliation;

2 the victim may assume blame for the abuser's behaviour and experience guilt or stigma at having raised a child (or married a spouse) who abuses;
3 fear of being removed from home and institutionalized;
4 the bonds of affection may be stronger than any desire to leave the situation;
5 concern about jeopardizing the family's status within the community;
6 societal views of the private domain of the family.

To these can be added Phillipson and Biggs' (1992) observations on factors affecting visibility of mistreatment in community settings, which include:

1 the reliability of neighbour and other community-based reports;
2 the willingness to report suspicions to formal services that might be seen as agents of control;
3 the question of intrusiveness into private living arrangements, especially when carers are not employees or subject to the norms of professional groups;
4 relations between minority groups and formal services;
5 frequency of contact between an older person and others who may comment on conditions;
6 communication between different agencies;
7 rural or urban location of service users.

Hall (1987) has noted that access to services might be especially difficult for ethnic elders suffering abuse. In this US study, the incidence of mistreatment was not found to vary with ethnic background; however, there was a marked absence of referrals to health and welfare agencies from these communities.

The reports above emphasize the difficulties that might be experienced by professional helpers, elders and their carers in addressing abuse and neglect across the public–private boundary. These difficulties, when added to potential problems associated with care management, may leave cases of suspected mistreatment open to collusion between professional helpers and families.

Collusive alliances

As noted earlier, care managers are under considerable pressure to maintain a partnership between themselves and carers, who are seen as the means by which older people are maintained in the community. The triangle of professional helper, carer and elder is thus the primary relation arising from community care. Like all triangular relationships it is inherently rivalrous, as there is always the possibility of two members pairing off, thus forming a collusive alliance that to some extent excludes the third party.

Biggs (1993b, 1994) has proposed that three possibilities for collusive alliance exist across public and private domains. First, the carer and helper may exclude the older person. This is referred to as task-based collusion, whereby the carer adopts a quasiprofessional role. It is a form to which community care would be most vulnerable. Second, carer and elder may ally against the professional helper through family solidarity. The danger would then be that the helper is allowed to monitor or support only on condition that he or she honorarily becomes a family member and does not bring mistreatment into the public domain. Finally, helper and elder might ally against the carer. The helper would heroically defend the elder whilst attempting to criminalize the carer.

This model emphasizes the active role taken by each party in constructing the meaning of mistreatment in any one set of circumstances. Reluctance to change often emerges from an absence of hope that active intervention will improve an existing situation. Effective helping would require that potential collusive alliances be recognized and action taken to clarify how the distinctive needs of each party might be met without resort to mistreatment.

Whilst the above reports go some way in exploring issues associated with mistreatment in domestic settings, they have yet to consider other forms of community-based abuse and neglect.

Community harassment

One of the consequences of an almost exclusive policy emphasis on abuse in domestic settings has been the relative absence of comment on community forms of abuse. Garrod (1993: 12) concludes from a UK study undertaken in Durham that 'Mistreatment is occasioned out with the family as much as within it and that mistreatment comes in many forms, with the most common being humiliation, harassment and theft or property misuse'. This is worthy of particular concern as the study addressed only community settings and thus did not include institutional abuse, where these forms of abuse might be less uncommon. The largest single group of perpetrators (at 27 per cent) were strangers, whilst in the majority of cases (59 per cent) the victim lived alone. The largest single category of reported mistreatment was harassment, at 32.8 per cent. Harassment was defined by example:

> For several months he had been the target for a local group of children who threw mud at his door, banged on his windows and frequently rang his doorbell before running away. This often occurred late into the evening. Despite several calls to the police the situation remained unresolved.
>
> (Garrod 1993: 11)

Pritchard (1993) reported incidences of 'gang abuse' as far apart as Sheffield and St Ives, Cornwall. She indicates that abuse is often organized and premeditated. Perhaps the most notorious case to come to judicial attention was of the murder of Edna Phillips by two 17-year-old girls, heard at Cardiff Crown Court in 1993. O'Hagan (1993), reflecting on his own childhood in Glasgow, points out that scapegoating of vulnerable older people was not uncommon.

Press coverage of the disability movement (*Rights not Charity* 1992) indicates a growing concern amongst the disabled community in Germany. Reports of up to 1,000 people having been subjected to physical and verbal assault, with abuse such as 'under Hitler you would have been gassed' and 'you are living off our taxes', were collected in one year alone. Whilst the latter would seem to constitute politically motivated scapegoating by adults, the British phenomenon seems to be largely caused by groups of youths and children.

The systematic harassment of older citizens bears considerable resemblance to forms of racial harassment. However, there would seem to be few records of the racial constitution of victim and perpetrator, nor for that matter of the ages of victims of racially motivated attack. An understanding of the links between forms of community-based harassment and their incidence in terms of age or other minority status is lacking. Where studies have focused on race as a dimension of mistreatment, the findings are almost exclusively focused on the characteristics of the perpetrator. Pan *et al.* (1992) found that in cases of spouse abuse, severe aggression was predicted by being black or Hispanic or by the use of drugs. Similarly, Stets (1990: 512) found that men who were severely aggressive were more likely to be young, black, and consume large amounts of alcohol. She concludes that 'Black men's aggressive behaviour may be more instrumental, perhaps to maintain control over their partner . . . since black men grow up in an environment where aggression is accepted, they may use it more to possess power'.

However, Gelles (1993) notes that whilst black and Hispanic groups are vastly over-represented in reported incidents of family mistreatment, this is most likely due to their visibility to protection agencies as groups with low income and high unemployment. Research thus runs the risk of simply reinforcing existing stereotypes. All of this research comes from the US and does not directly address elder mistreatment. Further research is needed in the UK and elsewhere to examine the causes of elder harassment, its relation to other forms of community violence and intimidation, and the development of community-based strategies to reduce marginalization and scapegoating in this context.

Conclusions

Our analysis of the relationship between caring agencies, families and community can be summarized as follows. Concepts of family and community are located in specific ways by social policy and political considerations to do with a moral understanding of the relationship between public and private space. An example from the early 1990s in the UK shows that policy on elder mistreatment might draw upon common-sense assumptions about the phenomenon that do not fit well with research evidence. This is most clearly the case when consideration is given to the role of carer stress, role reversal in families and suitability to care. These considerations make the professional task of negotiating boundaries between the public and private particularly difficult when it comes to issues of reporting, visibility and the possibility of collusion. Factors such as the existence of other forms of mistreatment, for example community harassment and the role played by power imbalance associated with marginalized groups, themselves become marginal to professional concern. It raises a number of points that should be taken into account if mistreatment is suspected in community settings.

First, the question of carer suitability, that it may not be appropriate for certain family members to care for their elderly relatives by virtue of family norms or personal characteristics, may be in conflict with dominant requirements of community care. This is especially the case if care management arrangements place exclusive emphasis on support to the carer as the means of maintaining an older person in the community. An assumption that caring is normal and natural might obscure the need for separate support to carer and elder, carer vulnerability and the presence of social problems or personal pathology underlying mistreatment. A focus on obligation, stress and inter-generational transmission would fit policy initiatives, but not the empirical evidence. Research results indicate that different categories of mistreatment, difference of degree of harm and different characteristics of families and communities should determine a discriminating approach to intervention.

Locating mistreatment within families would avoid consideration of other forms, which may be more common, such as community harassment and institutional forms of abuse, including institutional racism and gender bias. It also has the unfortunate consequence of associating mistreatment with unpaid care.

When mistreatment has been found to take place in domestic settings, workers should be aware of the tension involved in crossing the boundary between public and private space. This may lead to collusion of various forms, depending on the particular circumstances within any one setting. The objective for elder protection in domestic and community settings should be, on the basis of this chapter, to achieve a working solution that is based on each of the protagonist's needs, taking into account specific familial and cultural requirements.

6

Institutional care and elder mistreatment

Introduction

Whilst only a small percentage of older people live in some form of residential or institutional care, it has, perhaps, come to typify what many people think of when care for this group is considered. This chapter addresses the question of mistreatment in such settings, of which there is a considerable history in the form of injuries and scandals. Indeed, the question has been raised as to whether institutional care is abusive in itself. These and other issues are reviewed in this chapter, together with residents' views and social policy responses. We then consider what happens when institutions become abusive, including the influence of management strategy and workplace morale. A final section gives guidance on how non-abusive environments might be developed.

The character of institutional care

Institutional care holds certain special characteristics that distinguish it from life in the community and in domestic settings. Three of these have been outlined by Biggs (1993a). The first question concerns who generally inhabits institutional space. Typically, it includes two groups of people, residents and workers. The residents are there because they require certain services – the institution is effectively their home and their quality of life depends upon the sort of environment that is created and maintained. For staff, these buildings are primarily a workplace in which they perform the task of maintaining an appropriate environment in which a variety of caring functions can be performed. This fundamental distinction between the ways that an institution is conceived is often overlooked, and whilst in the best the two priorities complement each other in the service of meeting the residents' needs, things can go badly wrong if its management comes only to reflect the priorities of the second group. The quality of relations within the institution will depend upon how these groups interact both within and between themselves.

Second, it follows that, as Willcocks *et al.* (1987) have pointed out, elders are often expected to live their private lives in a public space. It becomes a private space insofar as residents live the majority of their lives within it and therefore require time and areas that protect their autonomy and privacy. It becomes a public space insofar as it is staffed and regulated as a working environment, which wider society has charged to manage the difficulties located there. The tension between public and private activity is often expressed as one between 'rights and risks' (Norman 1983), and is particularly acute in institutional settings because people usually come to live there when their attempts to maintain an independent lifestyle have broken down. Questions of autonomy become both psychologically and socially important when the needs of residents to maintain self-esteem clash with professional concern about safety and responsibility. Both reflect a need by both parties to be seen as coping with an inherently stressful situation.

Third, Biggs (1993a) points out that institutional residence highlights the question of the boundaries between a relatively contained world and the great outside. In other words, how far is an institution an open or a closed system? This refers to the way that boundaries between residence and community are negotiated, their flexibility and the expectations of the wider society on what and how contents, in the broadest sense of that word, are contained.

When compared with community living, institutional care provides a smaller, more manageable environment. It can contain a world that is relatively autonomous, with a life of its own, which may protect vulnerable individuals and provide a community of people with similar interests and requirements. However, these very qualities can also lead to secretiveness, suspicion of the outside and a lack of accountability. This tension is not helped by profound social ambivalence surrounding the role of institutional care. The act of providing a protective environment for residents may also protect wider society from taking seriously the social problems that are thereby hidden away from the public gaze. In the case of older age, Biggs (1989a) indicates that younger adults might also be avoiding intimations of some of the more unpalatable aspects of personal ageing.

Each of these tensions, between residence and workplace, between public and private space, and between open and closed systems, can be resolved to enhance the lifestyle of vulnerable elders. However, when the pressures of work, both personal and institutional, dominate residents' requirements, in a closed environment with scant respect for resident autonomy and privacy, mistreatment is always waiting in the wings.

A brief history of institutional inquiries

The history of British institutional care is littered with reports prompted by the discovery of mistreatment of elders. These include: Ely Hospital (National Health Service 1969), Besford House, Shropshire (Medd 1976); Moorfield, Salford (Hytner 1977); Stonelow Court (Derbyshire County Council 1979);

Nye Bevan Lodge, Southwark (*Independent* 1987); Camden Homes for the Elderly (Clough 1987); plus a number of registered-homes tribunal decisions (Brooke Ross 1987). The list includes National Health Service (NHS) hospitals, local-authority and private-sector establishments. It has prompted Glendenning (1993: 1), in a review of the literature on older people experiencing mistreatment, to comment that 'There is chilling evidence that these elderly people are more likely to be at risk than the 95% or 91% who live in the community'. Evidence from the USA has led Pillemer and Moore (1990: 318) to conclude that 'Abuse is sufficiently extensive to merit public concern and may be a common part of institutional life'.

Wardhaugh and Wilding (1993) have traced a pattern in the process of these investigations. Early inquiries often began from an assumption that the scandals uncovered were due to the corrupting influence of particular individuals: the 'bad apple' hypothesis. However, this approach was soon found to be inadequate as the extent of mistreatment became apparent. Explanations gave way to a more comprehensive critique of the nature of institutional care within these establishments. It is but a short step to conclude that corrupted establishments are themselves simply the most extreme examples of an entire rotten barrel: the nature of institutional care itself.

Are institutions abusive in themselves?

The argument that institutions are in some way inherently abusive has been put most forcefully in the work of the American sociologist Erving Goffman (1961) and by the Psychiatrica Democratica movement in Italy. Both critiques emerged from the field of mental health, but have had an influence across the spectrum of institutional care.

One perspective would suggest that institutions by their very nature abuse residents and brutalize staff. For example, Franco and Franca Basaglia (1988: 255) argue that:

> By distancing the patient from our world, we are uprooting him from his own world and turning him into an object which is isolated from its life history, from its environment and even from its own life. In fact he is simply reduced to the state of an object by our aggression.

It is claimed that the very presence of institutional care hangs above the heads of any who fail to pass as normal and is a threat against transgression of socially validated roles. Institutions are thus inherently discriminatory and serve to exclude from social participation those who cannot contribute to 'the dominant rationale of our culture, namely that of material production' (1988: 274).

This final point may be of particular importance to older age. Both Estes (1979) and Phillipson (1982) have drawn attention to the forcible exclusion of older people from working life through retirement, and to the fact that the poverty and the marginalization that so often accompany old age have their roots in a social rather than a biological construction.

The Psychiatrica Democratica movement resulted in Law 180, passed by the Italian government in 1978, which has led to the closure of institutions throughout that country. However, it soon became clear that financial considerations were playing a significant part in its implementation, whilst the social critique which underpinned it itself became marginalized.

Goffman's (1961) study of what he called 'total institutions' has had far greater influence on British and American policy. An academic discourse developed which both supported and systematized findings on successive scandals in the treatment of patients in long-term settings. In the British context, research by Townsend (1962) and Robb (1967) applied directly to the institutional care of older people. According to Townsend (1962: 79):

> In the institution people live communally, with a minimum of privacy, yet their relationships with each other are slender. Many subsist in a kind of defensive shell of isolation. Their mobility is restricted and they have little access to general society . . . they are subtly oriented toward the system in which they submit to orderly routine, lack creative occupation and cannot exercise much self-determination . . . the result for the individual seems fairly often to be a gradual process of depersonalisation.

Booth (1985) terms the result of institutionalization an 'induced dependency', which isolates residents both from current contact with the wider community and from their own pasts. This debate supported a shift in meaning of community care, with the focus on providing non-residential as opposed to just non-hospital care (Evandrou 1991). Whilst the alternatives to institutions have often been poorly thought through, residential care has become associated with an opposite, negative pole. This may partly be a result of its enclosed and protective nature and partly because of the positive value given to community, or more accurately 'independent' living. It is a line of thinking that can be traced through the Seebohm report (1968) to the National Health Service and Community Care Act 1990.

Users' views of institutional care

That institutional care is in some way seen as a negative potential future is supported by surveys of elders currently living in the community. Roberts *et al.* (1991: 119) note:

> One of the most prominent themes to emerge . . . was the extent of people's psychological and emotional resistance to the idea of residential care. Residential care is seen as something unpleasant – considering it is tantamount to accepting a dramatically reduced standard of life, to the point that it is viewed as a 'place to die'. For carers, considering residential care is equivalent to admitting defeat.

Campbell (1971) found, from a study of London elders aged 75 and over, that only five per cent were interested in residential care, whilst Salvage *et al.* (1986) found only 16 per cent of people questioned in Glamorgan were prepared to consider a residential option.

In an extensive review carried out as part of the wagner report, *A Positive Choice*, Sinclair (1988) notes that in two-thirds of cases, admission to residential care follows hospitalization or living in someone else's home. In many cases there was considerable pressure on elders to move elsewhere. He cites poverty, inadequate housing, increased disability and lack of appropriate community services as primary factors provoking admission. This combination of disadvantages has been described by Wilkin and Hughes (1987: 175) as a 'choice between an unpleasant battle to survive in their own homes and an equally unpleasant enforced dependence in the institution'. American research confirms this position. According to Hudson (1986: 156): 'Many would rather be at home and abused than in a nursing home. Indeed, most elders choose to stay in the abusive situation rather than face an unknown one.'

Criticisms of the concept of institutionalization

The assumption that institutional care is inherently oppressive has been challenged on a number of fronts. Sinclair (1988) indicates that researchers' criticisms of institutions as unnatural and unstimulating environments are not necessarily shared by elders actually in care. Institutions can provide comfort, physical security and freedom from worry, plus a mixture of privacy and companionship, which would not otherwise be available.

Baldwin *et al.* (1993) point out that critics all too readily assume institutionalization to be a uniform process and do not discriminate between different forms of residential care. Whilst Goffman (1961) was primarily interested in understanding how social control impinged on everyday life across a variety of settings, total institutions being but one, subsequent research has almost exclusively focused on institutional care. The latter is therefore lacking in comparative evidence. Baldwin *et al.* (1993: 75) comment that:

> In some parts of the country community services are highly routinised with set times for home helps and auxiliary nursing; social work intervention may be focused around narrowly defined and practically oriented activities, possibly linked to functional dependency rating scales, which give little scope to older people for independence and feelings of control. . . . In such circumstances depersonalisation, loneliness, withdrawal and depression may be common and might in other contexts be described as 'institutionalisation'.

These criticisms indicate that there may be more commonality between potential mistreatment in community and institutional settings than at first meets the eye. Abuse and neglect in institutional settings may be more visible precisely because it occurs in a predominantly public, albeit circumscribed, arena. Mistreatment in the community may take place in a private place surrounded by an anonymous outside world. The question of abuse and neglect by community services, as institutional responses to social need, has hardly begun to be examined (see Chapter 5).

Social policy and mistreatment

It is instructive, in the light of the above discussion, to look at social policy responses to elder mistreatment in relation to institutional care. As has been mentioned in Chapter 4, the year 1993 was important as a watershed in British professional awareness of elder abuse. Government guidance from the Department of Health Social Services Inspectorate (1993) to local authorities followed considerable media interest (*Community Care* 1993), and the setting up of Action on Elder Abuse as a national pressure group. However, no statements have been made about institutional abuse as the guidance referred only to domestic settings.

Phillipson (1992: 82) has noted that 'The identification of elder abuse as a form of family violence has led to an additional problem: the failure . . . to give proper weight to abuse in institutional settings'. This is not to say that the British state has failed to make a response to institutional poor practice. This has taken the form of concern about the quality of care existing in old people's homes, as exemplified in *Homes Are For Living In* (Department of Health Social Services Inspectorate 1989). This document includes a checklist and recording format organized under the headings privacy, dignity, independence, choice, rights and fulfilment.

Why, it is reasonable to ask, have these two settings of potential mistreatment been positioned so differently in terms of policy? It would appear that, on the one hand, abuse is seen as an exclusively domestic problem, whilst, on the other, institutional care is in need of encouragement and improvement. To understand this phenomenon it is necessary to place the growing recognition of elder mistreatment in the wider setting of transforming the British welfare state into a mixed welfare economy, a development that is ideologically satisfying to the right through the widespread privatization of residential and nursing care.

Reports from the USA indicate that an overwhelming concern with cost reduction and a market geared to investor-owned corporations, which tend to hire unskilled labour, would negatively affect conditions in caring institutions (Gilbert 1984).

In Britain, it may not have been politic to promote vigorous policing of a vociferous and politically sympathetic lobby during the late 1980s and early 1990s. Instead, it proved more palatable to restrict inspection of residential care to an enabling role, a sort of enterprise initiative for the welfare entrepreneur (Biggs 1987, 1991). This policy continued despite evidence from the United Kingdom Central Council for Nursing, Midwifery and Health Visiting (1994) that professional misconduct in nursing homes rose from 8 per cent in 1990 to 26 per cent of all cases in 1993. A second consequence of this policy was that the voice of the resident became increasingly marginalized, despite rhetoric to the contrary. This largely occurred as a result of a split between purchasing authorities and service providers. Reporting mistreatment may have become more difficult and certainly more indirect as a result. This policy has run in harness with the trend (Manthorpe 1993), following child protection procedures, whereby institutional care is seen as a place of safety. Institutionalization has often come to be seen as the solution to mistreatment in other settings.

What happens when institutions become abusive?

It can be seen from the above that whilst institutions have certain characteristics that make mistreatment a possibility, this may not be a problem unique to such settings. Some fulfil a valuable service, meeting expressed need. However, the question of how some institutions become abusive is worth further investigation.

Clough (1987), in his unpublished report to the Wagner Committee, cites a number of indicators of potential mistreatment. These have been summarized by Phillipson and Biggs (1992) as follows:

1 failure to agree within the managing agency about the purpose and tasks of the home;
2 failure to manage life in the home in the appropriate way;
3 when things went wrong, they were not sorted out;
4 poor quality and shortage of resources, particularly in respect of buildings and staff;
5 confusion and lack of knowledge about the guidelines around which the home was organized;
6 staff attitudes and behaviour;
7 staff capacity and lack of training;
8 low staff morale;
9 low status ascribed to the work;
10 failure by management to see a pattern of events – they treated individual instances in isolation.

Specific examples include complaints that occur over a long period and refer to more than one member of staff, poor hygiene (and the smell of urine), staff isolation and lack of supervision, residents seen as troublesome, and few visitors or outside contact. Counsel and Care (1992, 1993) has drawn particular attention to the use of restraint, both physical and chemical. Restraining patients or residents may be an especially sensitive measure of mistreatment, as it may be necessary to prevent injury, whilst also being convenient for the management of disruptive behaviour. The quality and severity of restraint would depend upon the general climate of the establishment in which it is used.

Many of the above indicators focus on management of the institutional environment rather than individual acts of abuse, which are often symptoms of a deeper malaise. Whilst paid carers who abuse may exhibit the same characteristics reported of abusers from other settings (see Chapter 7), 'The focus of an enquiry into violence should be not on the motives for violence, but on the conditions in which the usual moral inhibitions against violence become weakened' (Kelman 1973: 38).

Wardhaugh and Wilding (1993) point to a number of factors that might give permission to what they call 'the corruption of care'. These include:

1 the neutralization of normal moral concerns, whereby the resident is stripped of personal identity;
2 this is closely connected to the balance of power and powerlessness in organizations, whereby staff are simultaneously powerless as employees whilst having absolute power as 'carers';
3 the pressures of particular kinds of work, which include not only the unpleasantness of some forms of personal care, but also having to live with a

credibility gap between rhetoric from stated policy and the reality of difficult caring tasks;

4 management failure in terms of objectives, practice guidelines and mechanisms of accountability;

5 particular models of work organization that promote inward-looking and narrowed models of internal reporting; attention is drawn to the stifling of self-criticism and complaint, professional isolation, routinization and undue hierarchy.

When applied to care for older people, these factors have a telling ring. There is now a considerable literature that draws attention to the poverty of communication between many paid carers and elders in institutions. Giles and Coupland (1991) indicate that whilst elders wish for communication that is both affiliative and respectful, they often end up with professional behaviour that is marked by superficiality, a focus on limited, problem-based issues and a tendency to infantilize. Nussbaum (1991) found intergenerational communication to be 'quite controlled and unidirectional' during professional contact. Adelman *et al.*'s (1991) study found that physicians were more abrupt, condescending or indifferent to older people than to other adult patients. The best that Wilkin and Hughes (1987: 192) could describe from their study of residential care was: 'Formal politeness and an avoidance of personal contact which might invade the individual's right to privacy . . . the relationship was thus one of gratitude for services rendered, it was an instrumental relationship'. Similar findings have arisen in home-help provision (Leslie and Fowell 1988), nursing (Coupland *et al.* 1991) and social work (Jones 1986). These communication styles have led Biggs (1993b) to conclude that a combination of perceptions of old age in the minds of 'the not yet old', the absence of personal experience of old age to draw on, and the predominantly negative view of the potential contribution of elders to societal priorities, can make empathy especially difficult to achieve. In the worst, but by no means least frequent, of cases, elders are reduced to examples of 'type', as objects rather than beings with their own existential goals.

Inadequate attention to the transition to institutional care and its psychological effect on self-esteem, the importance of continuity, especially in terms of identity and personal possessions, plus the maintenance of identity within institutions once transition has been achieved (Tobin 1989), would increase the possibility that normal moral concerns for a fellow human being are reduced and negative institutional attitudes become endemic. Beginning to see elders as objects rather than human is the foundation on which a continuum of petty slights and abuses build into active mistreatment. Bennett and Kingston (1993) indicate in their research that 36 per cent of nursing staff had observed physical abuse in the preceding year, and 81 per cent had observed what they considered to be psychological abuse. A total of 10 per cent admitted committing one or more physically abusive acts, whilst 40 per cent admitted to psychological abuse. Kyser-Jones (in Monk 1990: 7) has grouped the most frequently reported complaints of staff abuse into four categories:

Infantilisation, treating the patient as an irresponsible, undependable child.

Depersonalisation, providing services in an assembly line fashion, disregarding the patient's individual needs.

Dehumanisation, not only ignoring elders, but stripping them of privacy and of their capacity to assume responsibility for their own lives.

Victimisation, attacking the older person's physical and moral integrity through verbal abuse, threats, intimidation, theft, blackmail, or corporal punishment.

At the extreme end of this continuum exist instances such as the events at Nye Bevan Lodge (*Independent* 1987: 5):

1 The incontinent were punished by being left unattended and shouted at. On one occasion faeces were shoved in the mouth of a resident by a 'care-assistant'.
2 One woman, crippled by arthritis, was upset by staff teasing her about the smell caused by her ulcerated leg. On one occasion the old lady said she was raped by a care assistant whilst being washed.
3 An old lady was found with burnt hands. She said she had been told to hold on to a towel rail. Faeces was later found embedded in her infected hands.
4 By contrast to the misery upstairs in the home among its old people there was a great deal of merry-making downstairs, among people mainly unconnected with the residents, after a bar was opened.
5 It seemed that the residents became an inconvenience on the ground floor and would be removed out of the lounge area to facilitate customers.

These reports prompted Vousden (1987: 19) to argue that:

It is self evident that when elderly and often confused residents are made to eat their own faeces, left unattended, physically manhandled, forced to pay money to care staff and even being helped to die, something is seriously wrong.

However, these revelations followed a fourth inquiry attempt amid media allegations of collusion within the local authority in question (*Independent* 1987). The events at Nye Bevan Lodge illustrate physical, emotional, financial and social mistreatment, with added allegations of institutional collusion at the highest level.

Workplace morale and mistreatment

Workplace morale emerges as a significant factor in determining the likelihood of the corruption of care for older people. Positive motivation is a significant factor in attracting workers to residential care. Studies from the US (Pillemer and Moore 1990) and from the UK (see Sinclair 1988) indicate that staff are less motivated by material aspects of the work than by humanistic concerns. For example, 96 per cent of respondents in the American study said that they were motivated because it is 'an occupation where you can help others'. However, this is not to say that working conditions, such as job security and the need for income (both noted by 49 per cent of respondents and rated as 'very much' a factor on a sliding scale), fail to be significant factors in maintaining morale.

High levels of stress and burn-out were reported as one of the most negative aspects of nursing homes revealed by this study.

Sinclair's (1988: 270) survey of British research concludes that 'there is no statistical evidence on the importance of staff (in older people's homes) comparable to that in the fields of child care and delinquency'. He cites altruism and the wish to work with elders, convenience of the job such as part-time working, plus need for employment and income as major motivators. Marked differences were found between conditions in public- and private-sector homes. Staff were more likely to be very young or themselves nearer retirement in the private sector than in the public. Sinclair (1988: 271) commented: 'Proprietor's needs to keep down costs meant that staff were often expected to work unscheduled overtime, and that their conditions of service were less satisfactory than in the public sector'.

Robertson (1991) found working conditions and relations with management to be important indicators of staff morale and quality of life for residents. Homes that engaged in active debate about equal opportunities and anti-discrimination were found to enhance resident self-expression significantly (Willcocks 1991), as would the promotion of anti-ageist attitudes amongst staff (Greenwell 1989; Biggs 1992; Biggs and Phillipson 1994; Hudson 1994).

Staff with positive attitudes to elders tended to recognize patterns of mistreatment earlier and also felt able to intervene (Lucas 1991). Archer and Wittaker (1991) found that if care staff were allowed time and energy for participation in thinking and planning the residential environment, both staff and resident wellbeing increased. Staff participation not only increased resident participation, residents becoming more 'critical and alive', it also reduced barriers and mutual blame between institutions. However, uncertainty about the future of the workplace, enforced reorganization and accompanying reductions in conditions and services were found to reverse the positive changes that had been achieved. Unfortunately, most researchers agree that the routinization of working practices, low pay and low status afforded by work with elders and inadequate training are by far the most common elements of such work (Phillipson 1982; Barr 1988; Sinclair 1988; Biggs 1993b). Wardaugh and Wilding (1993: 14) suggest that these conditions in the field of child care are precisely those 'which made residential care staff feel vulnerable and powerless and at the same time contributed to a climate within which abuses of power could easily take place'.

By that same token, the reduction of stress, increased job security, participation in positive decision making and conflict resolution plus regular and meaningful training would support those most positive motivations that staff report for entering the caring endeavour. Positive attitudes to elders would increase and the likelihood of abuse diminish. The above evidence would suggest that institutional abuse cannot be reduced to individual evil acts. The working environment and the relations that emerge between residents and staff are intimately related, and to change one without changing the other would be a fruitless exercise.

Throughout this book we have had reason to return to the fact that elders are people with civil rights, and as adults are as likely to act irrationally, even aggressively, as much as any other member of society. Violence to staff can be as much a part of institutional life as elder mistreatment, although one that is rarely brought to the surface. Pillemer and Moore (1990) report that only 11 per cent of staff had not been insulted or sworn at during the preceding year, and 41 per cent had been pushed, grabbed, pinched or shoved, whilst 70 per cent had been hit or had something thrown at them by residents. A study of staff working with elders in NHS establishments (*Community Care* 1993b) found 49 had suffered assault resulting in a visible injury. In 31 cases this had resulted in hospital treatment or time off work. Of 791 social workers questioned, 32 per cent had suffered physical violence; most common was verbal abuse, reported by 92 per cent. Violence was found to be most common in residential settings, reported by 48 per cent. Whilst these figures do not specify client group, they indicate a phenomenon of considerable concern.

Unfortunately, none of the studies report that staff were receiving training in conflict resolution. Of the social work staff, 23 per cent reported that no management support was received. Lack of attention to this aspect of institutional life would indicate an avoidance of mistreatment, which can then reproduce itself and be mirrored throughout organizational structures.

Putting things right

The first step towards resolving mistreatment is to uncover it. Elders living in institutions are notoriously reluctant to criticize the care they receive (Chiriboga 1990). This may be viewed as an 'unwillingness to bite the hand that feeds' (Wilkin and Hughes 1987). In many institutions, even the 'most minor of deviations from ideal compliance and gratefulness' are not tolerated (Tobin 1989). This has led to concern about the effectiveness of formal complaint procedures (Willcocks 1991) because once a culture of 'not letting on' develops it is extremely difficult to penetrate. A number of reasons militate against residents or staff blowing the whistle on malpractice, including power politics within establishments, denial or unwillingness to accept the validity of consumer critiques on the part of management, and fear of reprisal. Monk *et al.* (1984) found that over half of residents in their survey reported that they had refrained from making complaints. Indeed, it may be unreasonable to expect residents to complain without active support from staff, inspectors or citizen advocates. They are in the most vulnerable of positions, often being reliant on others to write, telephone or even articulate their experience as one of abuse or neglect.

Goffman (1963) draws attention to the culture that emerges amongst disadvantaged groups in receipt of care. Only two types of people could be trusted, the 'known' and 'the wise', in other words those with similar experiences to oneself and those who were capable of an empathic leap into what the experience of marginalization might be like. Seeing the humanity in others, in spite of their circumstances, plus a willingness to put oneself at the service of their requirements without interpretation or omission, is thus central to taking the role of ally and advocate.

The road to staff advocacy is by no means an easy one. First, many service users have already had a negative experience of professional indifference, tokenism or obfuscation as a result of attempting to contribute to decision making about their own requirements (Croft and Beresford 1992).

Second, staff may fear dismissal or disciplinary proceedings if they choose to blow the whistle on malpractice. Pressure to comply with existing practice has been emphasized by the Royal College of Nursing's (1992) campaign to expose poor practice and remove 'gagging clauses' in health workers' contracts of employment. The right of employers to silence staff concern was eventually supported at ministerial level.

Third, the risk is always run of being seen as a 'trouble maker' within the very working environment one is attempting to change. Attempts to improve practice may be met with resistance by colleagues immersed in the existing culture, leading to marginalization and even victimization.

Bender and Wood (1994) point out that 'whistle blowing' may over-emphasize the immediate act of disclosure without paying due attention to the lengthy struggle to get things changed and the personal stress that would result. They recommend that preparation, establishing influence based on a professional position, and maximizing freedom of movement (not being entirely dependent on one workplace) should be followed by a working strategy. The strategy would include: ensuring personal support outside work, support from trade unions and professional bodies; deciding on the degree of acceptable compromise in advance; and keeping detailed records (not just of poor standards of care but, equally important, ones indicating personal professional competence).

Whistle blowing encounters a number of problems that can be seen to reproduce the circumstances of elders subject to mistreatment. In the worst of cases, individual professional acts of disclosure may result in disbelief, indifference, persecution, and marginalization, in short, blaming the bringer of bad news. The bringer becomes located in the same space as the perpetrator insofar as attempts are made to expel them in the hope that the system itself will remain unharmed.

It is therefore essential to use existing channels and resources that are charged with ensuring the wellbeing of older people in institutional care. Most notable amongst these are duties given to inspection units. Brearley (1990: 197) notes that 'Any complaints system is only as good as the system for putting things right where there are found to be faults'.

People need to feel confident that something positive will happen if they do complain and, as has been argued above, this needs to go beyond the removal of an individual perpetrator to an examination of the policies and procedures, the climate, of the whole institution.

Phillipson and Biggs (1992) have supplied a checklist for social workers and homes inspectors in order to prevent abuse in residential homes. This includes the following.

1 If physical and chemical restraints are used, the reasons for using them should be constantly monitored and alternatives should be explored.
2 The physical environment of the home should be evaluated for its effect on residents' morale.

3 The extent to which the home encourages resident participation should be assessed.
4 Staffing ratios should be at a level which allows maximum stimulation for residents.
5 Staff training should be carried out on the issue of abuse and neglect.
6 Residential and nursing homes should develop an agreed policy on abuse and neglect.
7 Homes should have clear mechanisms for gathering consumer views about the quality of life inside the home.
8 Clear procedures should exist for ensuring that the collection of consumer views results in action on relevant items.
9 Advocacy schemes and charters of rights should be implemented inside homes.
10 Schemes for maintaining contact with informal carers should be devised.
11 Quality control and quality assurance mechanisms should be in place inside the home or long-stay setting.

To this might be added the fostering of citizen allies and advocates associations, independent of formal mechanisms, the members of which could befriend and support elders in care whilst ensuring regular contact is maintained with the wider community (Wertheimer 1993). Inspection visits should be both regular and visible to residents, with the specific opportunity for service users to make individual and collective representation to the inspector. As visits are likely to be infrequent, possibly at only six-monthly or even yearly intervals, codes of practice and avenues of complaint should be made clearly available to persons with sensory impairment or other disabilities. Means of access to them should also be clearly and easily achievable.

Central to the antiseptic of visibility is residents' participation in decision making. This has taken a particular form within the context of community care legislation. Means (1992: 3) distinguishes between two possibilities, which he calls the market and democratic approaches:

> The democratic approach would keep more services in the public sector but seeks to empower users by giving them a voice in services and thereby a chance to change (i.e. transform) their existing service or service organisation. In other words, if you don't like your day centre, you join your user committee and change it to your liking. . . .
> The market approach seeks to empower consumers by giving them a choice between alternatives and the option of exit from a service and/or provider if dissatisfied. Here the total pattern of provision is dictated by the sum of consumer choices – those services which are not chosen will go to the wall. In other words, if you don't like your day centre go to another one. Day centres which are unpopular will cease to trade.

One model therefore concentrates on the internal organization of the establishment, the other on choices between establishments. The latter relies on the existence of and information about alternatives, whereby the points of sale and exit become the primary opportunity for users to interact actively with services. Little emphasis has been given to the process of care within services, which might inhibit the detection of mistreatment and the promotion of quality care on a day-to-day basis. That purchasers are not the eventual users of services within the community care reforms, but groups of professionals and administrators, further excludes a user voice from the negotiating arena where decisions about contracting and compliance, and hence the process of care, take place (Biggs 1990a). This is in spite of evidence that users and carers are more concerned with the context of care than with points of entry and exit (Perring 1991).

Further, the emergent split between purchasing and providing services places another barrier between the regulation of a mixed welfare economy and malpractice in provider settings. Willingness to disclose instances of malpractice within a home may have a deleterious effect on marketing and even the continued funding of an establishment by the purchasing authority. It is therefore important that purchasers foster a climate in which providers can be honest about their difficulties without the immediate threat of closure arising. If self-disclosure is accompanied by clear objectives and deadlines for improvement, this may militate against the accompanying, but paradoxical, possibility of collusion between parties involved.

Whilst the development of inspection services is to be welcomed, the adversarial climate that often emerges if proprietors are challenged regarding the quality of care provided has led to a preoccupation with quantitative measures of care rather than qualitative ones. This is because it is easier to defend decisions based on inadequate safety precautions or overcrowding in front of a tribunal than it is the nature of interaction between staff and residents in all but the most grossly abusive situations. As the Registered Homes Act 1984 provides for de-registration only in the face of poor practice, it is often perceived as something of a sledgehammer to crack any shape of nut. It is therefore essential that, within this system, requirements for a process of participation within homes are addressed at the contractual stage and can be reliably monitored in accordance with those criteria.

Contracts between purchasers and providers of care allow the objectives of an establishment to be stated clearly. They also mean that agreements on progress between inspection visits can refer to undertakings specified in contractual terms. Specifications can thus begin to address qualitative issues such as those identified in *Homes Are For Living In* (Department of Health Social Services Inspectorate 1989), and the preventive measures identified by Phillipson and Biggs (1992).

Conclusions

Whilst some commentators have claimed that institutionalized care is in itself abusive, it has emerged that this is a matter of dispute. UK policy developments in the late 1980s and early 1990s have tended to concentrate on the improvement of care quality, rather than the active identification of mistreatment in residential settings. This is in spite of a growing number of inquiry reports and scandals indicating that when things do go wrong, they go wrong badly, with gross abuse of older people's human and civil rights.

Mistreatment in institutions spans a continuum from petty abuses in human relationships through to the excesses of Nye Bevan Lodge. Institutional cultures that have become abusive both permit and perpetuate individual acts of cruelty and exploitation. This permission that underlies individual acts of abuse means that it is not always self-evident that something is seriously wrong. Evidence is often of an indirect nature, covering management methods and patterns of systematic poor practice that have become common sense to those caught up in them.

These features contribute to the conclusion that service users' complaints are unlikely to be forthcoming in the light of institutional sanctions that might be applied. Similarly, 'whistle blowing' by staff may be a hazardous endeavour unless self-protective steps are taken in advance.

Openness to user participation within establishments, an active and independent advocacy network, and frequent contact with the world outside an institution would be positive signs that a non-abusive culture has developed. Workplace climate and morale have also been identified as key elements in determining whether mistreatment will take place.

In the next chapter we examine training interventions, their relationship to organizational change and the possible benefits that might result.

7

Training and elder abuse

Introduction

Training about elder mistreatment is becoming an increasingly important issue for health and welfare services. This has been prompted by a growing public and professional awareness of the problem as a result of a number of developments that took place in the 1980s and early 1990s. First, there is growing evidence of the prevalence (Ogg and Bennett 1992) and incidence (Garrod 1993) of abuse and neglect in the UK which complements findings from the US (Wolf 1992) and Canada (Podnieks 1989). Second, formal recognition of the problem by the Department of Health (1993) has prompted the emergence of local guidelines advising workers how to handle mistreatment (Penhale 1993). These require dissemination and checking that they are understood. Third, as research and practice wisdom has been accumulated, it needs to be shared and the implications for improved responses and prevention drawn out. Finally, training material has been made available that directly addresses the issue of mistreatment of older people in UK settings (Phillipson and Biggs 1992; Pritchard 1992).

These developments have been accompanied by a growing awareness that responses to elder abuse and neglect must take into account the special requirements of older people and their carers, which cannot simply be equated with existing service responses to child abuse or domestic violence. As practice and training experience accumulates, it has also become apparent that work on elder mistreatment brings with it a series of assumptions and emotional responses that, in the absence of proper training, supervision and organization development, may significantly affect the nature of decision making about it.

This chapter compares US and UK training initiatives. Principles are then outlined to cover clarity of aims and objectives, the question of ageism, the use of theory and the empowerment of older people themselves. The process of preparation, intervention and follow-up is then discussed with reference to educational and workplace settings. A final section looks at the relationship between training interventions and strategies for organizational change.

Training in the US and UK

The need for training was established by American research carried out in the 1970s and 1980s, as reviewed by Hudson (1989). Several studies recommended better training for professionals, with a strong educational component covering the ageing process in addition to detection of potential mistreatment. Many American research projects generated manuals and videos as a result. The growth of elder protection agencies gave further impetus to specific training programmes aimed both at helping informal carers develop coping skills (Scogin *et al.* 1989) and at specialist elder protection workers (Wolf and Pillemer 1994). A national survey, conducted by the US Administration on Aging (1993), indicated that whilst training was not as extensive as many practitioners would like, multiprofessional collaborations were taking place in significant numbers. The breadth of training included 'related professionals' such as administrators, bankers, as well as police/sheriffs, health and welfare workers.

In contrast, British initiatives on training have taken longer to develop. Biggs and Phillipson (1994) suggest three related reasons for this. First, they note an overriding concern with child protection and a concentration of resources in this area. This has led to a demand for postqualification social work training that has no parallel in elder protection. Second, the limited amount of indigenous research has led to a lack of awareness of the scale of the problem and limited scope for improved knowledge and expertise. Third, there has been, historically, a narrow scope of training for work with older people. What evidence there is suggests that the nature of such training is of variable quality, with traditional approaches to ageing (emphasizing issues related to sickness, frailty and disability) prominent at both qualifying and postqualifying levels (Phillipson and Strang 1986). The Central Council for Education and Training in Social Work has since added abuse of older people to guidance proposals for qualifying training (Winner 1992). Kingston (1994) has undertaken research to indicate whether such advice has been adopted by education providers. Ninety-five per cent of social work programmes indicated that elder abuse formed some part of their curriculum. This is less than for child abuse (at 100 per cent) but more than for domestic violence (at 85 per cent). Whilst it is impossible to come to any firm conclusions concerning the depth in which different forms of abuse are covered, these findings are encouraging. Reports for nurse training also indicate that elder abuse is taught to some degree. Ninety-eight per cent of respondents indicated that child abuse was included in curricula, with 81 per cent for elder abuse and 60 per cent for domestic violence. The figures for medicine are less encouraging, with 64 per cent for child abuse, 50 per cent for elder abuse and 35 per cent for domestic violence. These responses may change if US trends are followed, as there violence-related injury has become a major source of referral to health professionals (Berkovitz 1994).

To these observations can be added the fact that the growing status of elder mistreatment as a social problem has occurred in harness with a major restructuring of health and welfare services in the UK. Whilst the 1990 NHS and Community Care Act has increased concern about the welfare of older people and their carers in community settings, it has simultaneously focused the minds of strategic planners on issues of internal reorganization of existing services, both in practice and, by implication, through education. Training has often occurred at the same time as the development of practice guidelines, which has had the advantage of integrating awareness with new methods of working, but with the disadvantage that increased uncertainty about future working methods might detract from activity around 'yet another social problem'.

The training of workers in the field of elder abuse and neglect has therefore been subject to increased concern, but against a background of historical neglect of general skills for such work and considerable short-term restructuring of British service systems. These factors have affected the nature of training initiatives in ways that are different to developments in the US and Canada.

Principles for training programmes

Biggs and Phillipson (1994) have identified four guiding principles in developing training programmes: clarity about the aims and objectives of training; the development of an anti-ageist perspective; a grounding in theories that assist in understanding the complexity of issues arising through elder protection work; and a commitment to the empowerment of older people. Specific responses to cases of actual or suspected mistreatment should thus be based on an awareness of the social, cultural and institutional position of older people in society. Biggs (1992) has noted a tendency for some sponsors of training to dismiss the relevance of the social context of ageing in view of a concern to be seen to 'do something' about immediate and concrete events. Others have argued that responses of this sort may be a cultural characteristic of personal social service departments (Woodhouse and Pengelly 1991). However, it is argued here that unless workers, and the agencies they work in, understand contextual factors affecting the position and status of older service users, effective intervention in elder mistreatment is less likely to follow.

Clarity of aims and objectives

Clarity of aims and objectives should ensure that workers are sufficiently clear about the purpose of activity in what is a sensitive and difficult area. The first element requiring clarity concerns the value base of any intervention. This hinges on a recognition that older people should be able to live their lives free of violence and mistreatment in whatever setting – community, family, or institution – they are in. Distinctive moral and ethical issues need to be faced, particularly as adult–adult relationships require the consideration of conflict between professional judgement and service users' personal choices. There may not be a clear victim or perpetrator in many cases. In training terms, this would require that workers become aware of their own common-sense assumptions concerning older age, informal caring and the influence of age-specific priorities (Biggs 1993b).

The aims and objectives of training itself also need clarity. This is necessary to establish boundaries around the learning task and its implications for work beyond the training session. Clear boundaries will enable the training task to take place in a climate of relative safety of expression and an established understanding of expectations of outcomes. The importance of this becomes apparent given the uncertainty and anxiety that often surrounds elder mistreatment and, as was noted above, that training may be occurring at a time of service reorganization. At a personal level participants will need reassurance that feelings of inadequacy and discussion of mistakes, to learn from them, will be contained by the training group. The training contract should protect the facilitator from institutional pressure to deliver unrealistic results by clearly stating the focus and limits of any single intervention. Boundaries around stated objectives also help to ensure that accompanying institutional problems – for example the transfer of services to community settings, confusion over the role of carers and support services, competing priorities of different purchaser and provider agencies – do not eclipse a specific focus on mistreatment.

An anti-ageist perspective

One of the key ethical problems confronting work with older people is discrimination in society on the basis of age (Butler 1963; McEwan 1990; Bytheway 1994). An explicit anti-ageist framework arises from this as a priority for any training for work with older people. Work in this area has been developed by Itzin (1986) and Biggs (1989b), and has been reviewed by Biggs (1992). Itzin draws parallels between participants' experience of power inequality in childhood and the position of older people in adult society. Biggs has been concerned with relations between older people as service users and personal and institutional attitudes within service delivery systems. Typically, training would need to consider the impact of ageist attitudes on: interpersonal relationships with older people; the workers' own feelings about ageing and potential conflicts arising from this and, finally, the practices of major social institutions.

Ageism is seen as a mechanism for producing, sustaining and justifying abusive action towards older people, which would happen through infantilization, negative stereotyping and by determining institutional priorities and practices. Biggs and Phillipson (1994: 218) therefore maintain that:

Confronting ageism is central to understanding and confronting abuse and it is consequently important to maintain a clear link between the two on training programmes concerned with the mistreatment of older people.

Theoretical tools

Phillipson (1993) suggests that interactionist theory and theories of political economy will provide the basis for workers to understand some of the complex issues surrounding abuse and neglect. A number of writers have been working towards narrowing the theoretical gap between intergenerational behaviour on the one hand and social structures on the other (Estes 1979; Phillips 1989; Biggs 1993a; Bytheway 1994). This reflects a growing recognition that professional practice often has to reconcile social structural pressures in an interpersonal context. When addressing elder mistreatment the facilitator would have to decide the most appropriate way of introducing theory as a tool to understanding the process of abuse and neglect. Theories of elder mistreatment tend (as outlined in Chapter 2) either to be driven by practice in related fields – most notably child protection or domestic violence – or by the study of more general social phenomena that are then applied to that specific area. Both approaches hold advantages and disadvantages. Decisions on how to introduce theoretical material would depend upon its relation to existing organizational culture. This would include attitudes to conceptual development within any one agency (whether it has a reflective or instrumental attitude towards practice) and the traditional priorities of the agency (for example police may be more familiar with domestic violence, social services with child protection and citizens advice work with financial issues). Differences in audience, between professional workers, advocates, carers and older people themselves, will also determine how theoretical positions are understood and used. Whatever the context and audience, the introduction of theoretical tools should be judged in terms of the degree to which they facilitate greater breadth and depth of understanding, plus a greater flexibility of possible options and their reflective implementation.

Empowerment of older people

The final principle suggested by Biggs and Phillipson (1994) concerns the empowerment of older people. This applies both to an ability to hear what is being communicated in interpersonal settings and to the power and influence of elders as a group within the wider community. Training programmes therefore need to address the promotion of citizen advocacy (Wertheimer 1993), mediation (Craig 1992) and the development of self-help skills (Savo 1984). Implications for training are at least threefold. First, the training needs of volunteers and elders themselves would need to be addressed. Second, workers in formal services would need to be sensitized to new forms of collaboration with advocates and self-advocates, the principles underlying such work and an appropriate allocation of roles and functions. Finally, service users themselves may become trainers, requiring changes to established methods and resourcing (Biggs 1993b; Beresford 1994).

A consultation with older people, conducted by Action on Elder Abuse (1994), showed that, when asked, elders placed mistreatment within a context of reduced resourcing of services, ageism within health and welfare agencies and, as is also reflected in the Gray Panthers movement in the US (Kuhn 1977), the collective experience of service users across age barriers. Such perspectives would suggest that the challenge of mistreatment must be seen as addressing questions of social policy in addition to that of interpersonal problems between older people and their carers.

Training events

There are useful questions to ask whenever a training programme is being developed, which reflect considerations and preparation before the training event, process and content during training itself and, finally, follow-up once formal learning has taken place.

Preparation

Phillipson and Biggs (1992) have identified a number of issues that a facilitator should appraise when designing any intervention, in an attempt to add clarity to training and contribute to the eventual format of a programme. These factors will be briefly outlined. Questions of how the trainer came to be invited, by whom and whether the sponsor's view of the problem corresponds to that of the training participants will influence 'ownership' of the training agenda and thus the overall success of the enterprise. This implies that trainers should take care to consult widely on the proposed content of sessions. A training initiative will inevitably arouse expectations which may or may not correspond to the original training brief. The trainer will therefore have to have a clear grasp of the limits to their own intervention in terms of what can be offered, how much, and for how long. Questions surrounding the accessibity of information and to whom it goes will also be important at this stage. These points give important indicators about the situation the trainer is going to enter into and how her or his work will be received and used.

Preparation for the sessions would vary considerably depending upon the setting in which it was to take place, for example whether the trainer was asked to run a workshop with students who may not have had first-hand experience of working in abusive situations, or with a specialist team with a history of having worked together with older people. In the first case, the question of who has asked the trainer to teach is relatively unproblematic as systems for invited training are likely to be routine. Consultation on content would depend upon the existing curriculum and the knowledge students can be expected to have at that point in their training. If training is to take place with a team of professionals, within longstanding working relationships and in coordination with other services, the reasons for an intervention are likely to be much more hazy. Participants will already be embedded in organizational and managerial structures that would have influenced the decision to initiate training on elder abuse. This decision may also be related to specific events in the group's history, for example a particular case which has thrown up continuing difficulties in existing practice. The question of competing agendas around training or facilitation therefore takes on a higher profile in the minds of participants, if not the explicit reason given for training at this point in time. Consultation about content can therefore be an important factor in ensuring the commitment of participants and assessing the most effective means of intervention.

Concerns reported by potential participants might span both cognitive and emotional responses, as the following sample from Biggs (1994: 139–40) indicates:

a fear that if you champion elder abuse as a problem, you will be abused, blamed, victimised yourself; that disclosure is often not acted upon if it threatens informal caring arrangements; a concern with monitoring rather than personal intervention; anxiety at a perceived lack of legal power to intervene.

Additional information on the group's composition – such as gender balance, age range (particularly important in this context to assess current life goals and how these might affect attitudes to older age) and the need for interpreters, for example signers – can be gained either from course organizers or by questionnaire. Questionnaires to participants are a useful way of communicating the facilitator's interest in the learning group. They also allow questions of a confidential nature to be asked, such as whether individuals have had personal experience of abusive situations, and for the voluntary nature of participation to be underlined. Thus, expectations and the use to which training might be put would depend upon the mode of assessment that participants are subject to, whether they expect to practice in this area, their familiarity with the training methods that will be used, and in some cases personal or organizational agendas.

Although it is important to achieve a balance between the expressed needs of parties involved, facilitators would also have to judge whether the initial request reflects their own assessment of who needs training or consultation, where, and over what time period.

A final point about preparation concerns the facilitator's own position with respect to the intervention. Perceptions of the facilitator can be expected to vary depending upon whether he or she works for the same agency, a different but related one, or has external status. These factors will influence the degree to which operation as a 'third force', relatively independently of the issues outlined above, is possible (Nay 1978).

Training interventions

The preparation period will influence the eventual form that an event takes. It is generally helpful to classify types of intervention into two broad categories. First, there are technical interventions. These focus on a particular skill to be learned and might include assessing elder abuse (Breckman and Adelman 1988), communication skills with older people (Bender-Dreher 1987), or methods of working (Phillipson and Biggs 1992). Skill learning of this type would assume that the problem has already been examined and steps towards adaptive responding have been agreed. It may, for example, be that an agency has already decided to adopt a care management approach to elder abuse and simply requires operational expertise in that method. These types of intervention attempt to provide answers of the 'this is what you do' variety and rely on finding educators with sufficient specialist knowledge to implement them.

Second, there are interventions that attempt to address the processes evoked as part of elder protection work, the systems within which abuse has taken place and the forms of response currently adopted. An emphasis would be placed on facilitating the understanding of how practices have developed over time, the personal and institutional preconceptions at work and their consequences, in order to effect change in the service of more appropriate functioning. These interventions may take place over a longer time period, involve considerable organizational soul searching and have less tangible, though possibly more enduring, results.

It is likely that any training intervention that extends over a longer time period will be a hybrid in which questions affecting service systems feed back into the agencies, whilst specific technical needs will arise as deeper understanding of the problem emerges. The rest of this section will look at issues in running shorter, specified training events.

Group learning can hold a number of advantages for helping professionals when compared with individual tuition or formal lecturing (Biggs 1992). Exposure to diverse experiences and attitudes held by group members can serve to place often implicit guiding principles about 'normality' in a more relative context. This may be particularly important when considering behaviour in intergenerational relationships and notions of acceptable levels of conflict, where explicit norms are often tacit and unclear. Participants may also adopt roles that best suit their own personal style, whilst also learning from the styles and attempted solutions adopted by others. Groups, especially where they have a life outside the formal session, such as a work team, allow the formation of collective plans for action to take shape to support the generalization of lessons learned.

It is helpful for facilitators to think of any short-term event as being divided into a beginning, middle and end. At the beginning, especially if it is the first session of a series, participants will need time to 'ventilate', or talk about their reasons for coming, their previous experience and their particular views on elder abuse. If this opportunity is not allowed, misunderstandings and resentment may impede learning. It is also an opportunity for the facilitator to find out about group members and communicate that their own experiences and opinions will be taken seriously. During the beginning period the task at hand can be usefully explained, the trainer's role clarified and boundaries set around the purpose of the exercise. It might, for example, be necessary to clarify whether its purpose is to be personally therapeutic for participants, to focus on problem solving, or to rehearse specific professional skills. These considerations are particularly relevant to elder abuse, given the strong responses of blame, guilt, impotence, and the need for instant solutions or intellectualization that it can evoke.

The task, the use of particular training methods, is addressed in the middle period. During this stage the facilitator's job is to ensure that participants understand what they have to do and provide a framework to shape their ideas. Depending on the focus of the session, what is expected of participants will vary with respect to the 'rightness' of their practical activity. If, for example, the task addressed the correct use of assessment material, there may be specific procedures that have to be learned. If the task centred on attitudes, such as the different associations evoked by the labels 'abuser' and 'carer' (see Phillipson and Biggs 1992: 99–102), the acceptable latitude of personal opinion is that much broader. Indeed, the success of the exercise may depend on insight gained from some of the more unexpected responses.

At the end of a session, participants should have time to reflect on the task and share their insights and conclusions. Facilitators may need to take care that discussion is not dominated by a few vocal members, and intervene to ensure that a more representative picture emerges. If the session is part of a series, this period will divulge information on how the group is responding to elder abuse as a subject and the value of the training method being used. This can be used both to inform modifications to intervention or course design and also to give an indication of how far responses have changed across a series of sessions. It is important to bear in mind (sometimes in order to retain a modicum of self-worth as a facilitator!) that elder abuse can evoke a need to find the right solution quickly, or its opposite, despairing depression that the problem is insoluble. Both of these responses, which tend to reflect an unwillingness to dwell on the subject, can place the trainer under considerable pressure not to allow space for constructive reflection, either because it is not seen as directly relevant or because it brings participants closer to tackling a difficult and emotionally demanding situation. This is a particular difficulty when skill learning is addressed as it lends itself to the 'technical fix' which seems to offer a relatively undemanding solution in the short term, whilst leaving other issues unexamined, such as the process of interaction between a worker, an abused older person, and the abusing carer or paid worker. Given that the atmosphere in the learning group will also affect the facilitator/trainer, it is important to reflect on the meaning of feedback for the developing group process, as much as an indication that the whole programme needs to be thoroughly rethought. Undue flight into the latter can easily reproduce anxieties emerging from the group within the trainer's own planning. Reflection on those feelings left with the facilitator can, on the other hand, considerably deepen his or her understanding of the issues raised by abuse itself and thereby improve future sessions.

Consolidation

Different training formats allow different possibilities for follow-up, in other words, the degree to which learning can be consolidated after the formal input has finished. Follow-up is important because it will influence whether learning is generalized to other settings and sustained over time. Developing strategies for follow-up is easier if work has taken place with a committed team that continues to work together in the setting that learning took place. It is most difficult if participants have attended a short course away from their work setting, as isolated individuals who have then to return to an environment which is either unaware of or unwilling to recognize their new learning. A problem associated with work with older people, and abuse in particular, is the low institutional priority that is often given to this area. Both groups of former participants may find that mechanisms for responding are under-developed and subject to ageist assumptions. There is therefore a need to ensure that time is planned for, whereby workers can regularly review progress made, refresh knowledge and understanding, and find support from peers. In the case of isolated attenders of short courses, it may be necessary for consenting participants to exchange work addresses and telephone numbers. Training can also build follow-up days into the conditions of registration, to facilitate support and sharing of practice experience.

Whatever the constitution of the learning group, practice will be considerably enhanced by an environment that encourages reflective practice (Schon 1987). Reflective practice is considered to consist of three elements: knowing in action, reflection in action, and reflection in practice. 'Knowing in action' refers to an intuitive recognition of the nature of the main problems and whether a particular approach is likely to be effective. 'Reflection in action' allows the development of sensitivity and understanding of an activity whilst actually doing it. 'Reflecting in practice' involves looking back at why something worked, whether there are unresolved issues and whether the problem can be reframed to facilitate continued problem solving (Stevens 1994). The protection of such reflective space is considered essential for healthy personal and organizational development (Foster and Crespi 1994; Obholtzer and Zagier-Roberts 1994).

Wolf and Pillemer (1994) also emphasize, in the case of student practitioners in adult protection services, that the process of taking responsibility for cases of mistreatment should be gradual. Supervision should ensure that experience progresses from relatively uncomplicated to complex cases involving multiple types of mistreatment and service coordination problems. Research on training on elder protection for nursing assistants (Pillemer and Hudson 1993) found that training and support produced an improved attitude to residents, reduced conflict between residents and staff, and a reduction in abusive actions by both staff and elders themselves. Their conclusions reflect those of the US Administration on Aging's (1993: iv) survey, which recommended that 'The elder abuse/aging network . . . should put far more effort into ensuring that those who conduct trainings have well honed training skills'.

When training initiatives have been thought through, use skilled trainers, and are seen as part of the learning experience of the host agency, their impact can be significant.

These and the other issues cited above require examination of the organizational context of training intervention and continuing learning as an integral part of developing effective elder protection.

Organizational change

The impact of individual training initiatives largely depends upon the readiness of an organization to adopt new practices and modify its existing culture. It follows that considerable effort should be given to ensuring that training is integrated into strategic planning for organizational change. Such an approach has been promoted by the Department of Health in the general field of implementing the 1990 NHS and Community Care Act. It is suggested that initiatives should consist of three parts: short, medium and long term. Short-term agendas would include completing 'must dos', which are assumed to arise from changes in legislation or social policy, but might equally arise from increased awareness of a social problem. This phase would involve providing awareness training to all staff, identifying the learning needs of staff who will be operating new systems, and developing an immediate training response.

The second phase includes a stocktake of training delivered in order to identify gaps and monitor changes in working practices. Long-term strategy would include managing stability, growth and continued change. Emphasis is given to ensuring the commitment of senior management to strategic development at the beginning of any project, dissemination of policy into practice and ongoing monitoring to ensure that initiatives are understood and acted upon.

James *et al.* (1992) advocate the development of a 'diagonal slice', meaning people involved with each user group and at different levels of an organization who combine with users to form a project team to steer development work. The process of setting up the project would then mean that staff at all levels and users own the outcome of the exercise and that differences in perception facilitate planning rather than emerging as obstacles at a later stage. These authors place considerable emphasis on the process of organizational change and the early identification of key individuals within service systems who will promote initiatives. By recognizing informal as well as formal pathways to change, James *et al.* (1992: 19) identified 'mixers and fixers' who:

> Were people deliberately acting across line management and professional boundaries. What they appeared to be doing was spreading ideas and information across the organisation in a way often provided by staff development units. They were 'internal consultants' to their own department.

Change, James *et al.* (1992: 20) indicate, is often a matter of making headway 'not by imposing formal systems but by picking up, growing, expanding and eventually joining up quality work wherever it was to be found'. Change is therefore seen as an organic process; the task of development is to identify and nurture effective practice and to disseminate its influence elsewhere in the service system.

Increased concern about elder mistreatment often arises from a number of sources, including media coverage, practitioner-generated awareness, or changed statutory responsibilities such as a move to community-based services.

In the case of Tower Hamlets in East London (Wright and Ogg 1992), a significant policy and training initiative developed as a result of interest being shown by practitioners from a variety of backgrounds who work in different service settings (such as the local hospital, social services department, police and voluntary agencies). Initially, a forum for local interests and agencies was set up. This allowed contact networks to develop offering support and practical coordination of responses once cases of mistreatment had been identified. The forum was complemented by regular training events, which covered the social aspects of ageing in a multicultural society, recognizing abuse and neglect, ethical dilemmas, legislation and a multi-agency approach. Attempts were made to integrate training across agencies as part of a wider project to coordinate cook planning and develop operational procedures. After three years the forum was replaced by an annual conference to update practitioners on service developments and national issues (Wright 1993). Wright observes that as the initiative developed, practitioners became more aware of the differentiated functions required to respond effectively, that there was greater discrimination between types of mistreatment and between different levels of intervention appropriate for particular cases. One implication of the Tower Hamlets experience is that training needs to progress through a number of stages as the requirements of practitioners change. In the initial period, raising awareness of the issue, identification and establishing contacts, would dominate training objectives. During later stages trainers would need to become more responsive to specialized methods and issues arising from inter-agency collaboration as networks became established and practice wisdom accumulated. In Tower Hamlets a multiprofessional starting point reduced the danger of different institutions developing their own definitions and practices independently, which would then need to be untangled at a later date. Similarly, multiprofessional training allows practitioners from different backgrounds to reach a common understanding of the problem whilst learning about different institutional approaches and potential contributions that can be made. Informal interaction around training events creates opportunities to strengthen networking through getting to know opposite numbers and reducing the effects of institutional boundaries.

In the Tower Hamlets example, the parallel development of practice guidelines has enhanced the integration of training into strategic planning. Effective service development seems to have depended on the championing of the problem by key individuals in different service systems and a recognition of the interdependence of training and networking.

Conclusions

Whilst interest in elder protection training is growing, it is prone to being overtaken by other simultaneous agendas within agencies and training bodies. It is therefore important that trainers develop clear objectives and value positions for an intervention, most notably with regard to the sponsoring body itself. The context, whether in college or in a health or welfare institution, will have a significant effect on the nature and outcomes of training itself. Interventions may cover particular technical skills or the processes arising during elder protection and may be of a purely training nature or concern wider issues of organization development.

Research from the US has indicated that training on abuse prevention can have positive effects, not simply by reducing incidence but also by improving the general atmosphere between residents and workers. Examples from the British experience reinforce the message, arising from child protection, that multidisciplinary and inter-agency collaboration is a key factor in both training and organization development in this field.

Whatever the context, training should establish values concerning anti-ageist approaches, the empowerment of older people and its relationship to existing organizational systems. Trainers should familiarize themselves with the special characteristics of elder maltreatment. This would not simply require an analysis of 'the facts', important as this will be, but also an awareness of the complicated emotional responses that elder mistreatment can arouse and the ways that these can be reflected at different levels in organizations.

8

Interventions

Introduction

This chapter sets out some of the key issues to be considered when reviewing methods of intervention for tackling abuse and neglect. The framework for this discussion can be related to some of the points raised in Chapter 1. A key observation in that chapter concerned the move, in the post-war period, from a situation where abuse was scarcely acknowledged (at least within family settings), to one where it had become located within the broad area of family violence (Finkelhor and Pillemer 1988). We noted that it was possible to view this development as a product of the move from a position where abuse was 'contained' within dense kinship structures and large-scale institutions, to one where it took place within more fragmented kinship groupings, as well as relatively small-scale residential settings.

This sociological context is important in terms of understanding the possibilities for effective intervention to tackle abuse and neglect. For example, it is important to examine models of intervention which focus not just on the family in a narrow sense, but also on the broader networks of support within which people are enmeshed in the community. At the same time, these networks should be seen as having the dual capacity both to prevent as well as to generate abuse and neglect when faced with different circumstances and pressures. The overriding goal of intervention will be to work with the characteristics of particular kinds of social relationships and social networks, strengthening the available resources which may be used to ensure protection of vulnerable adults.

In examining the issue of intervention, the barriers and problems in this area will first be considered. The chapter will then explore a number of complementary models which are available for workers in health and social care settings. Finally, the chapter will consider future options in this area, focusing on some principles which can guide intervention in what is likely to become a significant area of social and health care practice.

Barriers to intervention

A number of obstacles have been identified in respect of intervention by professional workers in the health and social services. Penhale (1994) has identified five main issues. First, older people have the right to self-determination in all aspects of their lives. As a consequence, they may, when faced with the experience of abuse, refuse the offer of help from professional workers. Second, few options (particularly in the UK) exist in terms of proven intervention strategies. Workers operate with considerable uncertainty regarding how best to respond to some of the complex issues presented by abuse cases. Third, Penhale (1994) suggests that workers often respond to these difficulties by lowering their expectations about what can be achieved (part of a more general problem affecting work with older people). She suggests that this is especially likely in situations involving family violence or neglect of a longstanding nature. Fourth, the initial assessment may fail, for a variety of reasons, to identify the severity of abuse within the domestic or institutional setting. Finally, Penhale (1994: 144–5) makes the point that intervention may be an uneasy mixture of legal and therapeutic strategies:

> Most professionals are trained to 'cure' and not punish, so interventions that invoke the use of legal systems to provide redress or punish abusers tend not to be used. In any case it would appear that legal interventions will only really be considered by professionals if there is incontrovertible evidence that abuse has occurred. . . . [Moreover] elderly people and their carers have the right to refuse interventions in most situations; it is rarely possible to force people to accept interventions. Use of the legal system may therefore appear to be a rather extreme option, particularly if the evidence about the abuse is inconclusive. Practitioners may not wish to risk making a situation worse for an elderly client.

These barriers raise significant issues and are important to acknowledge in any discussion which attempts to encourage initiatives in this area. On the other hand, it is clear that the barriers may have been created in part because of the lack of clear principles or frameworks for guiding intervention. This chapter tries to move beyond simply listing the range of interventions which are possible. Instead, we shall examine the type of models which are available to workers, assessing these on a continuum moving from the least to the most restrictive forms of intervention.

Models of intervention

Despite the difficulties of intervention in the area of elder abuse, a range of possibilities have emerged both in debates and in care practice. It is helpful to organize the discussion around the idea of a number of complementary models available for guiding activity and intervention. These may be listed as follows:

1 the social network model;
2 the advocacy and mediation model;
3 the domestic violence model;
4 the social work intervention model;
5 the legal intervention model.

We shall now deal with each of these in turn, exploring some of the advantages and disadvantages associated with each approach.

The social network model

The starting point for the first model is the informal, non-institutionalized relationships which characterize many aspects of daily life. These are seen to take place across a wide geographical range, no longer bound by the densely knit communities once thought to be typical of many urban areas. Sociologists, for example, emphasize the diversity of social ties in contemporary life. Crow and Allan (1994) note that it is not that 'community-style' ties are absent; most individuals actively maintain a small number of significant informal bonds and regularly draw on these to help solve life's contingencies. However, such networks are rarely located exclusively within an immediate or bounded neighbourhood, and nor are they necessarily close knit or dense in the way that the traditional model of community suggests.

Clare Wenger's research has identified the importance of understanding the characteristics of social networks when assessing the type of support available to older people. Wenger (1994: 1) argues:

Research has shown that different patterns of informal support exist in the community. Different types of neighbourhoods have been found to produce different types of networks and different types of help-seeking behaviour. Various aspects of helping or support networks have been identified as critical. The most important of these have been found to be: (i) how close network members live to one another; (ii) how many members know each other and (iii) what informal sources are turned to for help. . . . Research has also shown that behaviour, including the search for support for help, is affected by the kind of social network that people have and that access to resources and the capacity to cope with problems is affected by the structure and the membership of the network.

A number of implications arise from the diversity of older people's social networks. First, there is the possibility that variations in the kind of networks in which older people are embedded may influence the likelihood of abuse and neglect occurring. Some older people are more vulnerable to abuse than others. But what translates the kind of risk factors outlined in Chapter 3 into the experience of abuse may be the constellation of actors supporting the older person. Older persons in isolated kin networks may be more at risk than older people involved in a network where there are a range of people – relatives, friends and neighbours – with whom they interact. Additionally, networks may vary greatly in terms of the likelihood that abuse will be recognized and acted upon.

Second, the idea of social networks may be important in terms of developing particular responses to abuse. Hooyman (1983) was an early advocate of this view, focusing on what she called the role of 'natural helpers' (friends, neighbours and relatives) in working with families to prevent abuse. Hooyman (1983) argues that few people are totally alienated or isolated. Even if neighbours do not have daily contact with an older person or their family, they may nevertheless know or suspect what is going on. Therefore, an approach based on identifying and strengthening natural networks may be highly significant. Hooyman (1983: 378) concludes:

> Professional intervention by [community nurses, social workers and others] . . . would focus on reducing the disruptiveness of caregiving by expanding or mobilizing the skills and resources of the part of the social network not already viewed by the family as a support resource. Such an approach can affect a large number of families with a minimum of effort and without increasing the family's dependence on formal services.

Such a strategy is not without its drawbacks. Many of the areas in which older people live may be experiencing the type of change (through population loss and the decline of services) which affect the potential for support from helping networks. In addition, these conditions (reflected in the pressures facing many urban areas) may be precisely those which leave older people vulnerable to abuse and neglect. The focus on networks, therefore, should also consider the issue of the conditions which might allow such networks to be strengthened and (where necessary) revitalized. This may involve wider questions concerning the political economy which affects the lives of older people, especially in terms of the localities and regions in which they live.

The advocacy and mediation model

The previous section considered the idea of social networks playing a supportive role in terms of assisting the care and support of older people. The idea of advocacy takes this argument a stage further by highlighting the importance of protecting the rights of older people. A number of factors have led to the growth of interest in the topic of advocacy:

1 the development of charters of rights (particularly in the field of residential care);
2 the problems facing informal carers, highlighted in a range of studies from the 1970s onwards (Twigg *et al.* 1990);
3 legislation such as the Disabled Persons Act 1986 and the NHS and Community Care Act 1990, which claim to give greater say to the consumers of services;
4 legal provisions such as guardianship and enduring powers of attorney;
5 the wider debate about the power of those professionals serving older people

(what Estes (1979) termed 'the aging enterprise') and the need to develop countervailing authority for older people and their carers.

In general terms, advocacy is concerned with the balance of power between the client as a member of a minority or other disenfranchized group and the larger society. From the advocate's point of view, the client's problems are not seen as psychological or personal deficits, but rather as stemming or arising from discrimination as regards social and economic opportunities. In consequence, techniques of intervention (in any area of work), rather than focus solely on individual clients, should challenge those inequalities within the system which contribute to or which cause difficulties for the older person (Phillipson 1993).

Definitions of advocacy have focused on many of the issues highlighted in the previous paragraph. Phillipson (1993: 183) cites the following as illustrative:

An advocate is one who organises activity to obtain goods, services, power or other resources for clients.

Advocacy is an attempt by an individual or group to influence another individual or groups to make a decision that would not have been made otherwise and that concerns the welfare or interests of a third party who is in a less powerful position.

Advocacy is a process of empowerment. Older people, by virtue of disability, frailty, marginalisation, institutionalisation, financial circumstances or even social attitudes, may find themselves in a vulnerable position where their ability to exercise rights is limited and their ability to exercise their rights or represent their own interests may be at risk. Good advocacy enables individuals or groups of people to have their interests given the same consideration as those of other citizens.

The advocacy perspective is of considerable relevance given the extent to which abuse may emerge from an imbalance of power, between carers and older people, in institutional as well as domestic settings. Given this, it is important to consider, as a first line of intervention, responses which attempt to restore power to the older person, and which may have a significant influence in eliminating the development of abusive situations.

The advocate's role may also be important in terms of assisting a broader range of initiatives to improve the quality of life of the older person. Filinson (1993), in an evaluation of an American programme of volunteer advocates for elder abuse victims, indicated its potential for more ambitious goal-setting, greater acheivement of goals and more extensive monitoring of carers.

The notion of advocacy raises the issue of developing forms of intervention which emphasize the right of self-determination for older people. Another concept using this principle is that of mediation. This idea has been used in the UK in the area of marital and family disputes, but in the US has been extended to work with older people. Craig (1994: 86) cites the work of Roberts, who has written extensively on the development of mediation work with families:

> He has been concerned about protecting people from what has been called 'the policing of families' . . . in which various social experts can, with the best (and sometimes the worst) of intentions, take over decision-making in situations of family conflict. Roberts developed a model in which the mediator is primarily skilled in facilitating communication and enabling disputing parties to exchange information and develop options from which they can choose their own future course of action.

As with advocacy, mediation offers a first (or minimal) level of intervention, and is most applicable to the early stages of conflict. In this context, it should be seen as a largely preventive measure, with the focus on the self-determination and empowerment of the older person.

This last point gives clues to the advantages as well as the disadvantages of advocacy and mediation as tools of intervention. The strength of these approaches is that they emphasize the participation of the older person in challenging the potential or reality of abuse. Moreover, they have particular value in the broader context of relationships between carers and older people. Hooyman (1983: 279–80) argues that most families probably have limited skills for providing continuous care to an older person. She concludes:

> In our society, cultural guidelines or specific norms for behaviour are lacking in intergenerational relationships. It is not very clear in our society whether families of older people are to feed, clothe, and take care of them on a 24-hour basis, in contrast to expectations regarding the care of young children. The media and a variety of handbooks all advise young parents about what to expect in caring for children, but such information is generally lacking for adult children attempting to care for elderly parents. Most families have few opportunities to rehearse the role of caregiver; they may hold unrealistic expectations for themselves and their older parents, which serve to increase the stress they experience.

These arguments confirm the value of an advocacy and mediation approach in trying to resolve some of the social and familial conflicts which may characterize the experience of abuse. The limitation of the model, however, is that its reliance upon participation and self-determination may, at least initially, be unrealistic. The older person may be reluctant (see below) to admit that abuse is taking place; if this is the case then advocacy and mediation may be resisted. More immediate measures may be necessary to protect and support the older person. Moreover, securing advocacy as an established practice raises a number of problems. First, it may not be viewed as a priority within the lead agencies organizing health and social care. Second, there may be insufficient people to carry out highly skilled advocacy and mediation tasks. Third, older people may themselves be unwilling to involve themselves in what may be confrontational settings.

In any event, although important as a possible model of intervention, advocacy will clearly need to be supplemented by other measures, especially those aimed at people at immediate risk of abuse.

The domestic violence model

This mode of intervention emerges from the work of researchers such as Finkelhor and Pillemer (1988), who have drawn comparisons between elder abuse and spouse abuse. These writers argue, first, that it is important to acknowledge that some elder abuse *is* spouse abuse that has sometimes been ongoing in a relationship for a number of years. In terms of older couples, age is certainly no barrier to domestic violence; indeed, the possibility of violence may be increased given some of the pressures experienced in later life. Pillemer and Finkelhor (1988: 250) go on to note that:

> even when abuser and victim are not husband and wife, the elder abuse situation is often more akin to spouse abuse than to child abuse: both parties are independent adults; they are living with each other by choice; the elder is connected to the abuser by ties of emotional allegiance and perhaps economic dependence, but certainly has more social, psychological, and economic dependence than a child would have.

The argument developed from the comparison between elder abuse and spouse abuse is that comparable forms of intervention are also possible. The type of provision suggested here would include: crisis intervention services; emergency refuges; support groups; counselling facilities; and legal expertise (Breckman and Adelman 1988; Hornick *et al.* 1992). Some examples of these have been given from the North American experience by Hornick *et al.* (1992: 321–2):

> The Victims' Services Agency in New York has instituted support and consciousness-raising groups for victims of elder abuse. A senior center in Winnipeg offers individual counselling for abused older people as do a few women's emergency shelters. Several states have special shelters for older abuse victims and several women's shelters do house older abused women.

The domestic violence model offers a way forward in terms of providing immediate protection when an abusive situation has been identified, and where there may be some reluctance by the older person to acknowledge the reality of abuse (Breckman and Adelman 1988). The advantage of the domestic violence model is that it offers some immediate strategies for the health or social care worker; it is also helpful in drawing links with other experiences of violence which may have affected people at previous stages in the life course.

The domestic violence model does, however, have a number of flaws. First, older people may find many of the options unacceptable, in particular the idea of moving out of their own home into a refuge or a residential home of some kind (indeed, this itself could be seen as a further violation of the rights of an elderly person). Second, it is not even clear that many of the options – such as using safe houses for battered women – are likely to be realistic. For example, the limited (mainly American) evidence on this suggests that very few women's shelters actually house older women or see them as an appropriate group for such facilities (Hornick *et al.* 1992; Vinton 1992).

The importance of the domestic violence model is that it points to the urgency of the situation which may face an abused elderly person. The response to this, however, may well need to be drawn from the broader repertoire of social work interventions, and it is to these that we now turn.

The social work intervention model

We have termed this the 'social work intervention' model, but it shares perspectives which are also used by health care and other professional workers. Integral to this model is the importance of case or care management as a strategy for handling some of the complex problems associated with elder abuse and neglect. Care management may be defined as a process of coordinating a range of support services into flexible packages of care to meet the assessed needs of the older person and the carer (Biggs 1993b). Despite the limitations of the care management model (see Chapter 7), older people who are vulnerable to abuse may derive particular benefit from an approach where one person takes responsibility for arranging a care package and for coordinating services into a home.

Within the care management process, workers may adopt a variety of techniques for assessing and supporting clients suspected of being abused. Specific assessment protocols have been developed (Fulmer 1984; Quinn and Tomita 1986; Breckman and Adelman 1988). Bennett (1990) notes that these protocols can be lengthy to complete but are thorough and should provide conclusive information regarding alleged abuse or inadequate care.

A helpful framework for developing responses to elder abuse is the staircase model developed by Breckman and Adelman (1988). The focus here is on overcoming the resistance which people may have to seeking help. Intervention is divided into three stages. The first is 'reluctance', a state marked by the victim's denial that the mistreatment has taken place. This is followed by 'recognition', a point where the victim recognizes that the problem is serious and cannot be managed alone. In the third stage, 'rebuilding', victims realize that they do not have to tolerate the mistreatment and can begin to shape their own lives. At all stages, it is clear that counselling will be a significant element in any intervention, and there is now an emerging discussion on the range of counselling skills appropriate for work with older people (Scruton 1989). Counselling should be with both the carer as well as the older person, and the worker may also consider more formal assessment tools to measure the pressure experienced by informal carers, the Caregiver Strain Questionnaire (Robinson 1983) being one such example.

Developing an approach to elder abuse from within conventional social and health care practice has two key advantages. First, it allows workers to draw upon established skills when responding to elder abuse. Second, and following from this, it places interventions as part of the core activities of generic health and social care: this may be important in preventing the marginalization of responses to elder abuse. The disadvantage is that initiatives on elder abuse may get 'crowded out' from the pressure of other demands on the time of professional workers. In addition, existing skills may prove inadequate in terms of identifying elder abuse. Abuse may simply be missed in conventional forms of assessment and care practice. This may be resolved only through developments such as specialist training (see Chapter 7) or the designation of groups at a local level with a specialist interest in elder abuse. An example of the latter is given by Rosalie Wolf (1992), where she describes the development, in the US, of community task forces to improve service delivery to abused and neglected older persons. Wolf (1994: 274) writes:

> These interorganizational structures bring together representatives of many different sectors of society including law, medicine, nursing, social services, mental health, aging, religion, criminal justice, law enforcement, financial management and adult protective services. They have been responsible for identifying service gaps, establishing new programs, educating the public and professionals, and advocating for legislative changes to improve the system.

Structures along these lines would seem an important step forward in the case of Britain and may eventually emerge from some of the discussions around procedures for handling abuse which are being developed at local and regional levels (see below).

The legal intervention model

The issues raised by elder abuse have already led to calls for more substantial powers of intervention to protect vulnerable older people. The Law Commission (1993) has published a paper setting out what statutory powers might actually look like, and groups involved in the campaign on elder abuse are pressing for a review of the legal area (*Community Care* 1993a). The question of greater legal powers again raises complex issues and brings out fundamental questions about the rights of both older people and those involved with their care.

The first point to make is that there already exists substantial legislation relevant to the protection and support of older people. This varies from service-oriented legislation such as the 1990 NHS and Community Care Act and the 1984 Registered Homes Act, to protective legislation such as the 1983 Mental Health Act. In addition, criminal legislation, such as the Offences Against the Person Act 1861, the Matrimonial Homes Act 1983, and injunctions available under the law of tort, may also be relevant in cases of abuse (Department of Health 1993; Griffiths *et al.* 1993).

There is also domestic violence legislation which may be used in cases of abuse, including the Domestic Violence and Matrimonial Proceedings Act 1976 and the Domestic Proceedings and Magistrates Court Act 1978. Ouster orders (1976 Act) or exclusion orders (1978 Act) are available either to exclude one party from the matrimonial home or to allow access to the other party who has been wrongly excluded. Non-molestation injunctions and personal protection orders may also be used where violence has been used or threatened (Morley 1994).

Given the available legislation, we need to ask what prevents it from being used and whether new legislation (such as specific powers aimed at the frail elderly) would be any more effective. Griffiths *et al.* (1993) have given three reasons for the current difficulties. First, some legal procedures, particularly criminal prosecutions, are inappropriate in many cases of elder abuse, because the perpetrators of the abuse are themselves victims of the situation (for example, carers subject to an excessive degree of strain and pressure). Second, legal procedures are often under-used because of negative attitudes or lack of expertise on the part of professionals such as lawyers and social workers. Third, the concept of abuse is seldom conceptualized in legal terms. It is doubtful whether any of these problems would change – they may in fact be exacerbated – by the introduction of a new set of statutory powers. Moreover, it must also be said that new legislation would be pointless without a significant commitment of resources – both social as well as legal. Unfortunately, we already have many examples where major legislation has been introduced (such as the 1986 Disabled Persons Act), only to be rendered ineffective through the failure to commit sufficient funds for full implementation.

Many reports do of course cite the American experience of adult protective legislation, suggesting that this has given significant support to vulnerable elders (Department of Health 1992). However, the evidence from the US is that in the absence of supportive services, legislation can actually do more harm than good, resulting in unnecessary institutionalization and premature separation of the older person from the carer. The criminalization of abuse and neglect would seem to be a pathway to be avoided at the present time. A more appropriate response is for increased resources to health and social services to extend their work in the field of adult protection in general and the area of elder abuse in particular.

Conclusions

This chapter has identified a range of models which may be helpful for dealing with cases of abuse and neglect. Specific areas of intervention are important in institutional settings, and some of these have been discussed in the preceding chapter. In terms of looking at the way ahead, six points should be stressed.

First, intervention in the area of abuse should guard against further erosion of the rights of older people. It is essential in this regard to start wherever possible from the older person's perception of the problem, together with an understanding of his or her own life history (Phillipson and Biggs 1995).

Second, we need to take seriously the point raised by Hooyman (1983) concerning the lack of guidelines for handling care between generations. This may be seen as part of a wider phenomenon reflected in the 'negotiated' nature of care arrangements (Finch and Mason 1993). There are no clear and binding rules which govern the giving and receiving of care. It is precisely for this reason that it is important not to pathologize the carer who commits abuse, but to develop sensitive but effective forms of social intervention.

Third, carers, older people and workers should each be seen as contributing resources towards a potential solution to abuse. Part of the problem in cases of abuse is that people feel trapped in a situation without hope of a better alternative. If workers are not to collude with such situations, it is important to recognize a variety of power imbalances and negotiate a solution acceptable to each party.

Fourth, improved resources will be crucial in terms of resolving many of the issues discussed. For example, Chapter 6 reviewed some of the problems in residential care, and suggested a number of procedures for combating abuse. But it will be difficult to ensure that these are in place, whilst there is a situation in which nearly half of social services departments in England and Wales fail to meet the statutory requirement of visiting homes at least twice a year; in some cases councils are even failing to visit homes once a year (*Independent*, 17 October 1994). In addition, the funding crisis in community care itself places older people at risk of abuse, with the withdrawal of key services which may be vital in ensuring that their support network is able to maintain them in their own homes.

Fifth, significant progress is being made in the UK in the construction of practice guidelines and procedures. These are being developed by an increasing number of statutory bodies, with some cooperation between local authorities and health authorities. Such developments are matched at a national level with the emergence of organizations such as Action on Elder Abuse. Progress along these lines indicates the gradual maturation of the debate on elder abuse, with greater awareness amongst key actors at local, regional and national levels.

Finally, intervention will need to be guided by key principles for supporting workers who take action over abuse and neglect. The following points are illustrative:

1 Workers should be encouraged to be vigilant about the possibility of abuse/neglect whilst being aware of the fact that there are no clear criteria for identifying abused elders and few interventions that are totally acceptable to all the parties involved.
2 Shared decision making is essential. Sharing should be conducted both by involving a range of professional workers in developing a strategy for tackling abuse and by ensuring that workers are supported in the decisions they make about protecting vulnerable elders.
3 Departments will need to develop policies which empower older people in situations where they lead marginal lives. Policies for tackling abuse must therefore be concerned with advocacy and strengthening self-care abilities in later life.
4 The goal of work in the field of abuse should be ensuring that older people enjoy a life free of violence and mistreatment. This will require intervention and vigilance in a range of settings: at a macro-social level in terms of social attitudes and beliefs about older people; in the care provided by paid and unpaid carers; and in the environments of nursing and residential homes. A comprehensive policy on mistreatment will need to address all these different levels of abuse if it is to be fully effective.

The points reviewed in this chapter indicate the importance of developing a major debate about the way forward in terms of handling the problem of abuse. This chapter has tried to indicate the range of possibilities open to health and social care workers. Other lines of action are possible and innovation in this area is certainly needed. A major issue will be whether the barriers to intervention reviewed at the beginning of this chapter can be overcome. The evidence here would suggest some optimism, with the emergence of an important debate in the 1980s concerning the need to develop an anti-ageist social work practice, and the need to promote advocacy and empowerment amongst groups such as older people (Biggs 1993a).

Set against this are pressures which may limit the scope of social intervention, these ranging from constraints on the resources available for community care, to low expectations amongst those delivering formal provision. Resolving these tensions will be crucial if effective responses to abuse are to be devised. The framework presented in this chapter should be seen as a starting point for the discussion which will be needed to ensure greater protection for older adults in the community.

9

Conclusion: The challenge of elder abuse

Introduction

This book has attempted to set out some of the issues and concerns which are beginning to arise in the field of elder abuse and neglect. The view has been taken that maltreatment is a complex phenomenon, reflecting a number of different pressures and constraints affecting older people. Arising from this observation, this book has had a dual purpose: first, to map out an area which is beginning to be identified as significant in both the research and social policy arenas; second, to say something about the difficulties associated with talking about abuse and neglect. How do we define the problem? How is its existence best explained? What are the different reasons for abuse – in institutional in contrast to family settings? On what basis could effective interventions be made?

Such questions give clues to the sociological problems which surround the question of abuse. In this chapter, an attempt will be made to draw together the different strands of the argument pursued in this study. In doing this, some specific proposals will be made for tackling the conditions which give rise to abuse and neglect. The starting point in the chapter will be current debates in gerontology itself and the lessons these hold for understanding the existence of the mistreatment of older people.

Perspectives on ageing

In the 1980s, significant developments took place in academic thinking about later life. In the area of social theory, there was the emergence of 'critical gerontology' and the beginning of a reassessment of the contemporary situation of older people. Social construction or political economy theory focused upon structural pressures and constraints affecting elderly people.

Researchers emphasized divisions and inequalities associated with class, gender and ethnicity, and the impact of these on the lives of older people (Minkler and Estes 1992). The political economy approach also questioned what Estes and Binney (1989) termed the biomedicalization of ageing. This was seen to have two closely related aspects: the social construction of ageing as a medical problem; and behaviours and policies growing out of thinking of ageing as a medical problem. According to Estes and Binney (1989: 588):

> Equating old age with illness has encouraged society to think about aging as pathological or abnormal. The undesirability of conditions labelled as sickness or illness transfer to those who have these conditions, shaping the attitudes of the persons themselves, and those of others towards them. . . . Sick role expectations may result in such behaviours as social withdrawal, reduction in activity, increased dependency, and the loss of effectiveness and personal control – all of which may result in the social control of the elderly through medical definition, management and treatment.

From the humanities, emphasis was placed upon the absence of meaning in the lives of older people, and the sense of doubt and uncertainty which seemed to pervade their daily routines and relationships (Moody 1992). In the culture of the late twentieth century, older people, it was argued, seem excluded from authority and relationships which could provide security in their lives. According to Thomas Cole (1992: 237):

> We must acknowledge that our great progress in the material and physical conditions of life has been achieved at a high spiritual and ethical price. Social security has not enhanced ontological security or dignity in old age. The elderly continue to occupy an inferior status in the moral community – marginalized by an economy and culture committed to the scientific management of growth without limit.

Cole goes on to stress the urgent need to review the place of older people in society, and argues that we should recognize the importance of developing a new sense of the meanings and purposes of the last half of life. Biggs (1993a) has extended this argument, pointing out that elders have requirements which can form the basis for alliances in common with other groups in society *and* requirements that are special to their place in the life course. Both would need to be included if the debate on ageing is not to 'ghettoize' our most senior of citizens and address their particular circumstances.

An additional debate, one which emerged from outside social gerontology, has been the concern with generational equity. This discussion has challenged the legitimacy of older people as a worthy group benefiting from economic and social support (Phillipson 1990). In this perspective, the old are pitted against the young in the competition for resources. The consumption of the former is seen to have the potential to dwarf the productivity of the latter, with the possibility of a reduction in living standards for future generations (Preston 1984; Thompson 1989). Neo-conservative governments in the 1980s 'talked up' the possibility of conflict, suggesting that workers were 'reconsidering' how much they should pay in taxes to support pensioners (Phillipson 1990). Increasingly, people were asked to think of their own old age rather than that of others (or other generations), and accept that they would have to rely upon a different kind of welfare state (Johnson *et al.* 1989). These trends would serve to polarize the interests of different generations and would hold implications for the status of older people as full citizens in society. It is our contention that the citizenship of older people should be reinforced, rather than diluted by policy and practice. This would mean that elders' interests are seen as an essential component of what it means to be participating adults. Policy initiatives should, without exception, consider the implications for the civil and human rights of older people at the point of formulation.

An abusive society?

The different arguments presented from these approaches to the study of old age have clear significance for debates which are concerned with the maltreatment of older people. The implications are that abuse and neglect may be derived from an environment of cultural and economic ambivalence towards older people. Arguably, abuse has the potential to thrive if the meanings attached to later life are unclear. Equally, abuse may develop if the resources received by the old are insecure and open to challenge. More generally, the norms and values which sustain abuse are encouraged by social trends which present the old as a marginal group; which encourage a language of generational division; and which fail to give a sustaining vision to the third and most especially the fourth age (Cole *et al.* 1993).

This framework of social ambivalence has, from a historical perspective, been a continuing theme in the lives of elders (Minois 1989). But the contradictions and uncertainties seem even more striking in our own times: first, because of the surge in importance, especially in the post-war period, in ageing populations; second, because of the availability of resources which *could* secure and stimulate the lives of elderly people. Both these observations point to the importance of 'talking down' the language of abuse which emerged in the 1990s, and, instead, revitalizing the meaning and purpose of later life.

This last point represents a major proposition we would put forward in this conclusion: namely, that the conditions which sustain abuse will be removed only by the development of a stronger and more secure vision for old age. Three examples might be given to provide a way forward on this issue. First, a starting point for protecting people from mistreatment of all kinds must lie in giving greater recognition to the significance of their lives, and the importance of their own memories and experiences for the community as a whole. Lessons can be learned from such experience together with a greater understanding of how current conditions have come about. Telling a life story is seen to be an essential part of retaining personhood in later life (Bornat 1994). Recognition of this in fact serves a dual purpose: for the storyteller it extends the field of control and self-expression in their lives – the basis of either preventing abuse or stopping it. For those who may commit abuse, it places the person in a wider context which may challenge the marginalization which abuse represents. The argument here is that people are vulnerable to abuse when they are seen to be on the edge of communal life. Restoring older people to the centre – through recognition of the uniqueness of their lives and the contribution which they continue to make – is a fundamental strategy for challenging abuse. Again, it is essential to see older people as citizens with civil rights that are honoured in practice as well as in policy. Forms of mistreatment would need to be placed in this wider context if the dignity and perspectives of older people are not themselves to be abused as protective interventions take place.

Second, it is clear that a new approach is needed for describing the relationship between generations. The intemperate language of the 1980s, which drew upon longstanding metaphors focusing on the burden of old age (Warnes 1993), served to legitimate the climate of abuse affecting older people. An alternative language would emphasize the interdependency of generations (Phillipson *et al.* 1986). This perspective would acknowledge ageing as a public concern to be shared equally across the life course. Above all, we should not 'off-load' the responsibilities for an ageing population to particular generations or cohorts – whether old, young, or middle aged. Ageing is an issue *for* generations, but is also to be *solved* with generations. The pressures which lead to abuse may be precisely those which arise from a debate which seeks to limit the extent of shared responsibilities. Identifying ageing as a communal issue also requires that we acknowledge the accountability of all groups in preventing abuse from occurring. Professional work in abusive situations would need to recognize the intergenerational nature of both problems that arise and the solutions that can be achieved (Biggs 1994).

Third, a theme related to the above concerns challenging the idea that older people face inevitable dependencies arising from biological and physiological change as they move through the life course. Older people do experience profound changes to the body which raise many issues for the quality of their lives. However, the way in which society responds to these changes is of crucial importance. In our society, people are given full accreditation as human beings only when they have reached a relatively high level of cognitive, emotional and biological development. This aspect of how human development is perceived has major implications for older people. Featherstone and Hepworth (1989: 261) suggest that:

> If the process of becoming an acceptable human being is dependent upon those developments, the loss of cognitive and other skills produces the danger of social unacceptability, unemployability and being labelled as less than fully human. Loss of bodily controls carries similar penalties of stigmatisation and ultimately exclusion. Deep [or late] old age is personally and socially disturbing because it holds out the prospect of the loss of some or all of these controls. Degrees of loss impair the capacity to be counted as a competent adult. Indeed, the failure of bodily controls can point to a more general loss of self-image. . . . The loss of bodily controls also impairs other interactional skills, and the loss of real power through decline in these competencies may induce others to feel confident in treating the individual as a less than full adult. Carers may, for example, feel secure in the belief that the person 'inside' will not be able to return to wreak any vengeance on them whatever their former social status or class background.

Changes to the human body may, therefore, be a crucial agent in creating the conditions for abuse and neglect and for disturbing social interaction between older people and those involved in their care. This has important implications for the prevention of abuse, focusing on the need to consider the way in which developing perspectives which challenge ageist assumptions about disability and frailty could be a liberating approach to challenging abuse itself (Bytheway 1994).

An additional issue arising from the theme of dependency concerns the way this is socially constructed (Estes 1993). The basis of this approach has already been spelt out in Chapter 5, where the notion of older people being affected by different forms of social discrimination was discussed. The implication of this approach is that abuse may arise from the way in which older people come to be marginalized by society (and by the services which they are targeted to receive). If people are predisposed to abuse elders because of their biological dependency, the likelihood of this is increased through social forces which discriminate both against older people as well as those involved in their care (Biggs 1993a; McEwan 1989). Such a perspective would suggest that the challenge to abuse must be seen as concerning a broad range of social policy issues, as well as focused social work with families and individuals.

An abusive family?

As well as general social issues, we need to consider particular institutions which have an important role in the lives of older people. The role of the family has been discussed at various points in this book and a number of specific issues are raised by some of the ideas discussed. In Chapter 1, we noted the move from a position where abuse was 'contained' within relatively dense kinship structures and large-scale institutions, contrasting this with the development of more fragmented kinship groupings and small residential homes. In this context, abuse of older people in the late twentieth century represents something of a paradox: a public issue of concern for many professionals and activists who have constructed it as a new social problem (see Chapter 3), yet, at the same time, an issue which may be experienced at a very private level within one's own home (Chapter 5) or in an anonymous residential care setting (Chapter 6).

The argument from this book is that the debate on abuse will not move forwards unless clearer links are made between these public and private domains. The public discussion and analysis of elder abuse reflects wider themes about the changing nature of social care in general, and family support in particular. The phenomenon of family violence has always been rooted in the norms and conditions surrounding family care and this may be especially true in the case of groups such as older people. It may be that the emergence of abuse as a social issue has coincided with increased uncertainty about the way in which care relationships are to be handled. Community care policies suggest a degree of social consensus about how support for older people should be managed. In contrast, researchers such as Finch and Mason (1993) remind us that the rules governing help from kin are highly variable and subject to complex forms of negotiation. This would suggest that in some cases abuse may be bound up with the contradictory pressures and expectations that are placed upon the family: by the tension between the social pressure to provide care, and the obstacles people may face in achieving this.

A major link, therefore, between the private and public debates about abuse concerns how generations care and support each other. In this context, concepts such as maltreatment and abuse need to be used with some degree of caution. Abuse in fact, though a lived experience for some older people, may also be a metaphor for the way in which families are changing in terms of care preferences (Phillipson 1994). Care for older people is *not* defined by any clear social norms (in contrast to care for children). It thus follows that our definition of abuse is equally uncertain (as was highlighted in Chapter 3). But the reasons are not just that older people are adults and hence supposedly in control of their lives, but also that issues of who should provide care and under what terms are in a state of flux. The idea of abuse may be an expression of this uncertainty as much as it represents the real experience of older people. This does not, of course minimize the importance of abuse at an individual level; it does, however, indicate the complexity of abuse as a social issue.

The concept of citizenship would aid us in establishing a balanced perspective, sitting, as has been argued in Chapter 2, at the crossroads of social status, interpersonal relations and personal dignity. It could point towards an agreed means of negotiating transactions between public and private space, which reminds the helper that each party has certain rights and requirements. As such, citizenship provides a unifying factor that can be applied across differing perspectives, plus a basis on which negotiation between parties can begin. This debate would extend notions of abuse and neglect beyond the confines of abusive families to include questions such as community harassment and institutional mistreatment.

Abusive institutions?

In Chapter 6, a number of issues were discussed relating to the situation of people in residential settings, where the problem of abuse has been identified in numerous reports over the past 30 years. This area is likely to continue to raise difficulties, given the rapid growth in the private sector market. This has moved from providing just 50,000 nursing home and residential care places in 1967, to nearly 200,000 in 1994. Growth on such a scale has clearly raised issues about the quality of care provided, and the risks to which vulnerable elders may be exposed.

These concerns are reinforced by doubts about the framework regulating this type of provision – the 1984 Registered Homes Act. Brammer (1994), in a major review of the Act, raises a number of criticisms which have important implications for the prevention of abuse in such settings. Her criticisms include: first, there is no clear definition of who is a 'fit' person to run a home – despite the key role of this term within the registration process, fitness is nowhere defined in Act nor even the subject of guidance; second, the legislation is framed in paternalistic terms and gives insufficient emphasis to the rights of residents; third, resources to ensure proper implementation of the Act are inadequate. As was noted in Chapter 8, inspection units are invariably understaffed, thus compromising the effectiveness of the regulation and inspection process. Brammer (1994:436) makes the following points in concluding her article:

> The Registered Homes Act in its current form is deficient in a number of respects. . . . [For example] insufficient guidance given to inspection officers; the limited legal sanctions available; and the tendency of the tribunal to favour the private sector entrepreneur. . . . In order that residential care can be seen as a positive choice, and not simply as a last resort, standards need to be raised beyond the level described by one homeowner who stated: 'It was a good home. No one died and no one was taken to hospital'. In the long term this area must be seen as part of the wider problem of treatment and attitudes towards the elderly and form part of a comprehensive review of the law in that area.

Historically, institutional abuse and neglect most readily spring to mind when questions of elder mistreatment are raised. However, as our research for this book has shown, it has recently become an area of relative neglect in the priorities of policy makers, researchers and theorists. Future study of elder abuse could do considerably worse than provide a conceptual framework that takes the changing nature of institutional care into account, one that goes beyond the walls of any one hospital or residential home. Institutional abuse could then be viewed as part of a broader perspective encompassing abusive systems of care and control.

Concluding comment

This chapter has identified both general as well as specific policy issues for responding to the question of abuse and neglect of older people. It has been indicated that the question of abuse does raise both fundamental issues about the place of older people in society, and questions of social and welfare practice. This, it might be argued, is the most important conclusion to emerge from this book: namely, that the condition of abuse is inseparable from a wider concern about the status of older people and the language used to describe their relationships within key social institutions. Challenging abuse will require, to some degree, reconstructing many aspects of the relationships older people experience within the family, in residential homes, and in other community settings. A social policy is needed which addresses the question of how older people can live lives that are free from violence and mistreatment. Our argument suggests that such a policy should begin from a consideration of the conditions under which all older people in society live, and placing maltreatment within that context. An exclusive focus on the most deprived, and the prejudices that thereby receive support, have resulted in the paradoxical situation whereby abuse can be recognized whilst very little is done to prevent it.

In raising citizenship as a unifying force in this debate we hope that this book will make a contribution to policy, research and practice. In terms of policy, the potential effects on the status of older citizens should always be considered before a final position is achieved. This would include both an analysis of ways in which draft legislation might prejudice the existing rights of elders as a group *and* how elder mistreatment is positioned as a social concern. Exclusive concern with mistreatment might eclipse other, equally relevant problems that older people face.

In terms of research, a perspective is needed that explains the complex nature of abusive situations on at least three levels. This should take account of the personal, interpersonal, and the socially constructed nature of mistreatment. It is not enough simply to categorize types of abuse and neglect, although this is a valuable starting point. It is also important, first, to unpack the ways that different conceptions of abuse emerge and how behaviour is influenced. Second, we must also examine the systems that perpetuate and reproduce mistreatment at each level and how these levels interact. In writing this book we have become painfully aware of the thinness of current knowledge. Research that is adequately controlled, most notably by comparing abusive and non-abusive situations, is rare and this needs attention both from funders and from ethical committees.

Practice intervention should start from the premise that older people can be active participants in the project of achieving lasting solutions, either by self-activity or through the use of nominated advocates. Placing citizenship at the top of this agenda would require that any intervention, however well meaning, must consider the implications for enhancing an elder's ability to negotiate requirements from a position of equality in circumstances where power is distributed unequally. The position and contribution of agencies to power imbalance should be critically assessed if abuse at the level of caring (formal and informal) is not to be reproduced at other levels of the helping system. Abusive situations emerge between adults with different agendas who have often lost hope that alternative ways of living can be achieved. The role of the professional helper would be to contribute to a mutually acceptable future, free from maltreatment from whatever source.

These are important challenges, but ones which, if tackled effectively, will do much to transform the lives of elderly people at risk of abuse.

References

Aber, J. and Zigler, E. (1981) Developmental considerations in the definition of child management. *New Directions for Child Development*, 27 May.

Action on Elder Abuse (1994) *Newsletter*. Mitcham: Age Concern.

Adams, D. (1988) Treatment models for men who batter: a profeminist analysis. In Yllo, K. and Bograd, M. (eds), *Feminist Perspectives on Wife Abuse*. Newbury Park: Sage.

Adelman, R., Greene, M. and Charon, R. (1991) Issues in physician–elderly interaction. *Ageing and Society*, 11: 127–47.

Alliance Elder Abuse Project (1983) *An Analysis of States' Mandatory Reporting Laws on Elder Abuse*. Syracuse: Catholic Charities.

American Public Welfare Association/National Association of State Units on Aging (1986) *A Comprehensive Analysis of State Policy and Practice Related to Elder Abuse: A Focus on Role Activities of State Level Agencies, Interagency Coordination Efforts, Public Education/ Information Campaigns*. Washington,DC: APWA/NASUA.

Anderson, M. (1974) *Family Structure in Nineteenth Century Lancashire*. Cambridge: Cambridge University Press.

Anderson, M. (1985) The emergence of the modern life-cycle in Britain. *Social History*, 10(1): 69–87.

Anetzberger, G., Korbin, J.E. and Austin, C. (1994) Alcoholism and elder abuse. *Journal of Interpersonal Violence*, 9(2): 184–93.

ARC/NAPSAC (1993) *It Could Never Happen Here*. Nottingham: NAPSAC.

Archer, L. and Wittaker, D. (1991) *Improving and Maintaining the Quality of Life in Homes For Elderly People*. SWRRU, University of York.

Austin, C. and O'Connor, K. (1989) Case Management: components and program contexts. In M. Peterson and D. White (eds), *Health Care for the Elderly*. New York: Sage.

Baker, A. (1975) Granny bashing. *Modern Geriatrics* 5(8): 20–4.

Baldwin, N., Harris, J. and Kelly, D. (1993) Institutionalisation: why blame the institution? *Ageing and Society*, 13: 69–81.

Bardwell, F. (1926) *The Adventure of Old Age*. Boston: Houghton, Mifflin.

Barr, H. (1988) *Training for Residential Care*. London: CCETSW.

Basaglia, F. (1989) Italian reform as a reflection of society. In S. Ramon and M-G. Giannichedda (eds), *Psychiatry in Transition*. London: Macmillan.

Baumann, E. (1989) Research rhetoric and the social construction of elder abuse. In J. Best (ed.), *Images as Issues: Typifying Contemporary Social Problems*. New York: Aldine.

Beachler, M.A. (1979) 'Mistreatment of elderly persons in the domestic setting'. Unpublished manuscript, Brasoria County, Texas.

Bender, M. and Wood, R. (1994) When nightmares come home: maintaining one's integrity in unacceptable places. *Clinical Psychology Forum*, 63: 5–9.

Bender-Dreher, B. (1987) *Communication Skills for Working with Elders*. New York: Springer.

Bennett, G. (1990) Action on elder abuse in the '90s: a new definition will help. *Geriatric Medicine*, April: 53–4.

Bennett, G. and Kingston, P. (1993) *Elder Abuse: Concepts, Theories and Interventions*. London: Chapman & Hall.

Beresford, P. (1994) *Changing the Culture: Involving Service Users in Social Work Education*. London: CCETSW.

Berger, P. and Luckman, T. (1966) *The Social Construction of Reality*. London: Allen Lane.

Berkovitz, N. (1994) 'Community care in the U.S.' Conference paper: International Perspectives on Care in The Community, London School of Economics, July 1994.

Best, J. (1989) *Images as Issues: Typifying Contemporary Social Problems*. New York: Aldine.

Biggs, S. (1987) Local authority registration staff and the boundary between public and private care. *Policy and Politics*, 15(4): 235–44.

Biggs, S. (1989a) Professional helpers and resistances to work with older people. *Ageing and Society*, 9: 43–60.

Biggs, S. (1989b) *Confronting Ageing*. London: CCETSW.

Biggs, S. (1990a) Consumers, case management and inspection: obscuring social deprivation and need? *Critical Social Policy*, 30: 23–38.

Biggs, S. (1990b) Ageism and confronting ageing. *Journal of Social Work Practice*, 4(2): 49–65.

Biggs, S. (1991) Community care, case management and the psychodynamic perspective. *Journal of Social Work Practice*, 5(1): 71–82.

Biggs, S. (1992) Groupwork and professional attitudes to older age. In K. Morgan (ed.), *Gerontology: Responding to an Ageing Society*. London: Jessica Kingsley.

Biggs, S. (1993a) *Understanding Ageing*. Buckingham: Open University Press.

Biggs, S. (1993b) User participation and interprofessional collaboration in community care. *Journal of Interprofessional Care*, 7(2): 151–60.

Biggs, S. (1994) Failed individualism in community care: the case of elder abuse. *Journal of Social Work Practice*, 8(2): 137–50.

Biggs, S. and Phillipson, C. (1994) Elder abuse and neglect: developing training programmes. In M. Eastman (ed.), *Old Age Abuse*. London: Chapman & Hall.

Block, M. and Sinnott, I. (1979) *The Battered Elder Syndrome*. Maryland: University of Maryland Press.

Blumer, H. (1969) Fashion: from class differentiation to collective selection. *Sociological Quarterly*, 10: 257–91.

Blumer, H. (1971) Social problems as collective behaviour. *Social Problems*, 18(3): 298–306.

Booth, T. (1985) *Home Truths*. London: Gower.

Bornat, J. (ed.) (1994) *Reminiscence Reviewed*. Buckingham: Open University Press.

Bornat, J., Phillipson, C. and Ward, S. (1985) *A Manifesto for Old Age*. London: Pluto.

Bowker, L. (1993) A battered woman's problems are social, not psychological. In R. Gelles and D. Loseke (eds), *Current Controversies on Family Violence*, Newbury Park: Sage.

Brammer, A. (1994) The Registered Homes Act 1994: safeguarding the elderly. *Journal of Social Welfare and Family Law*, 4: 423–37.

Branson, N. and Heinemann, M. (1971) *Britain in the 1930s*. London: Heinemann.

Brearley, C. (1990) *Working in Residential Homes for Elderly People*. London: Routledge.

Breckman, R. and Adelman, R. (1988) *Strategies for Helping the Victims of Elder Mistreatment*. London: Sage.

Bristowe, E. and Collins, J. (1989) Family mediated abuse of non-institutionalised frail elderly men living in British Columbia. *Journal of Elder Abuse and Neglect*, 1(1): 45–64.

Brooke Ross, R. (1987) *Registered Homes Tribunal Decisions*. London: Social Care Association.

Brown, H. and Craft, A. (1989) *Thinking the Unthinkable: Papers on Sexual Abuse and People with Learning Difficulties*. FPA Education Unit.

Burston, G. (1977) Do your elderly patients lie in fear of being battered? *Modern Geriatrics*, 7: 20–4, 54–5.

Butler, R. (1963) The life review. *Psychiatry*, 26(1): 895–900.

Butler, R. (1985) *Why Survive? Being Old in America*. San Francisco: Harper & Row.

Butler, R. (1987) Agism. In *Encyclopaedia of Aging*. New York: Springer.

Bytheway, B. (1994) *Ageism*. Buckingham: Open University Press.

Campbell, M. (1971) Study of attitudes of nursing personnel toward the geriatric patient. *Nursing Research*, 20: 147–51.

Cantor, M. (1983) Strain amongst caregivers. *The Gerontologist*, 23(6): 597–604.

Challis, D. and Davies, B. (1986) *Case Management and Community Care*. London: Gower.

Chiriboga, D. (1990) The measurement of stress exposure in later life. In K. Markides and C. Cooper (eds), *Aging, Stress and Health*. New York: Wiley.

Cicirelli, V. (1986) The helping relationship and family neglect in later life. In K. Pillemer and R. Wolf (eds), *Elder Abuse*. Dover: Auburn House.

Cicourel, A. (1973) *Cognitive Sociology*. London: Penguin.

Clough, R. (1987) Unpublished report to the Wagner Committee on Residential Care.

Cole, T. (1992) *The Journey of Life: A Cultural History of Aging in America*. Cambridge: Cambridge University Press.

Cole, T., Achenbaum, A., Jakobi, P. and Kastenbaum, R. (1993) *Voices and Visions of Aging: Towards a Critical Gerontology*. New York: Springer.

Commonwealth Office for the Aged (1993) Recognition of, and responses to, the need for elder protection in Australia. *Australian Journal on Ageing*, 12(4): 24–31.

Community Care (1993a) Elder abuse campaign. *Community Care*, 1 July.

Community Care (1993b) Violence toward social workers. *Community Care*, 7 October.

Counsel and Care (1992) *What if They Hurt Themselves?* London: Counsel and Care.

Counsel and Care (1993) *The Right to Take Risks*. London: Counsel and Care.

Council of Europe (1992) *Violence Against Elderly People*. Brussels: Council of Europe.

Coupland, J., Coupland, N. and Granger, K. (1991) Intergenerational discourse. *Ageing and Society*, 11: 189–208.

Craig, Y. (1992) Elder mediation. *Generations Review*, 2(3): 4–5.

Craig, Y. (1994) Elder mediation: can it contribute to the prevention of elder abuse and the protection of the rights of elders and their carers? *Journal of Elder Abuse and Neglect*, 6(1): 83–96.

Croft, S. and Beresford, P. (1992) The politics of participation. *Critical Social Policy*, 35: 20–44.

Crow, G. and Allan, G. (1994) *Community Life: An Introduction to Social Relations*. London: Harvester Wheatsheaf.

Crystal, S. (1986) Social policy. In R.S. Wolf and K.A. Pillemer (eds), *Elder Abuse: Conflict in the Family*. Dover: Auburn House.

Dalley, G. (1988) *Ideologies of Caring*. London: Macmillan.

Decalmer, P. and Glendenning, F. (1993) *The Mistreatment of Elderly People*. London: Sage.

Derbyshire County Council (1979) *Report to Social Services Committee: Stonelow Court Aged Persons' Home*. Matlock: DCC.

Department of Health (1993) *No Longer Afraid: The Safeguard of Older People in Domestic Settings*. London: HMSO.

Department of Health Social Services Inspectorate (1989) *Homes Are For Living In*. London: HMSO.

Department of Health Social Services Inspectorate (1992) *Confronting Elder Abuse*. London: HMSO.

Department of Health Social Services Inspectorate (1993) *No Longer Afraid: The Safeguard of Older People in Domestic Settings*. London: HMSO.

Dobash, R. and Dobash, R. (1992) *Women, Violence and Social Change*. London: Routledge.

Dollard, J. (1939) *Frustration and Aggression*. Newhaven: Yale University Press.

Douglass, R., Hickey, T. and Noel, C. (1980) *A Study of Maltreatment of the Elderly and Other Vulnerable Adults*. Ann Arbor: UMP.

Dowd, J. (1975) Aging as social exchange. *Journal of Gerontology*, 31: 584–95.

Eastman, M. (1982) Granny battering. *Community Care*, 413: 27.

Eastman, M. (1983) Granny battering, a hidden problem. *Community Care*, 27 May: 11–13.

Eastman, M. (1984a) *Old Age Abuse*. Mitcham: Age Concern.

Eastman, M. (1984b) Honour thy father and mother. *Community Care*, 26 January: 17–20.

Eastman, M. (1988) 'Granny abuse'. *Community Outlook*, October: 15–16.

Eastman, M. and Sutton, M. (1982) Granny battering. *Geriatric Medicine*, November: 11–15.

Emerson, R.M. and Messinger, S.L. (1977) The micro-politics of trouble. *Social Problems*, 25(2): 121–34.

Estes, C. (1979) *The Ageing Enterprise*. San Francisco: Jossey-Bass.

Estes, C. (1993) The aging enterprise revisited. *Gerontologist*, 33(3): 292–9.

Estes, C. and Binney, E.A. (1989) The biomedicalization of ageing: dangers and dilemmas. *Gerontologist*, 29: 587–96.

Evandrou, M. (1991) *Challenging the Invisibility of Carers*. London: London School of Economics.

Faulkner, L. (1982) Mandating the reporting of suspected cases of elder abuse: an inappropriate, ineffective and ageist response to abuse of older adults. *Family Law Quarterly*, 16(1): 69–91.

Featherstone, M. and Hepworth, M. (1989) Images of ageing. In J. Bond, P. Coleman and S. Peace (eds), *Ageing in Society*. London: Sage.

Fennell, G., Phillipson, C. and Evers, H. (1988) *The Sociology of Old Age*. Buckingham: Open University Press.

Filinson, R. (1993) An evaluation of a program of volunteer advocates for elder abuse victims. *Journal of Elder Abuse and Neglect*, 5(1): 77–94.

Filinson, R. and Ingman, S.R. (1989) *Elder Abuse: Practice and Policy*. New York: Human Sciences Press.

Finch, J. (1984) Community care: developing non-sexist alternatives. *Critical Social Policy*, 9: 6–18.

Finch, J. (1989) *Family Obligations and Social Change*. Cambridge: Polity Press.

Finch, J. and Mason, J. (1990) Filial obligations and kin support for the elderly. *Ageing and Society*, 10(2): 151–78.

Finch, J. and Mason, J. (1993) *Negotiating Family Responsibilities*. London: Routledge.

Finch, J. and Wallis, C. (1993) 'Inheritance, care bargains and elderly people's relations with their children'. Paper to Annual Conference of the British Gerontological Society, Kent.

Finkelhor, D. and Pillemer, K. (1988) Elder abuse: its relation to domestic violence. In G. Hotaling, D. Finkelhor, J. Kirkpatrick and M. Strauss (eds), *Family Abuse and its Consequences*. Newbury Park: Sage.

Fischer, D.H. (1989) *Albion's Seed: Four British Folkways in America*. New York: Oxford University Press.

Formby, W.A (1992) Should elder abuse be de-criminalised? A justice system perspective. *Journal of Elder Abuse and Neglect*, 4(4): 121–30.

Foster, A. and Crespi, L. (1994) Managing care in the community. *Journal of Social Work Practice*, 8(2): 169–84.

Froggatt, A. (1990) *Family Work with Elderly People*. London: Macmillan.

Fulmer, T. (1984) Elder abuse assessment tool. *Dimensions of Critical Care Nursing*, 3(4): 216–20.

Fulmer, T. and O'Malley, T. (1987) *Inadequate Care of the Elderly*, New York: Springer.

Garrod, G. (1993) The mistreatment of older people. *Generations Review*, 3(4): 9–12.

Gelles, R. (1993) Through a sociological lens: social structure and family violence. In R. Gelles and D. Loseke *Current Controversies on Family Violence*. Newbury Park: Sage.

Gelles, R. and Straus, M. (1979) Determinants of violence in the family. In W. Burr, R. Hill, F. Nye and L. Reiss (eds), *Contemporary Theories About the Family*. New York: Free Press.

Gelles, R. and Loseke, D. (1993) *Current Controversies on Family Violence*. Newbury Park: Sage.

George, J. (1994) Racial aspects of elder abuse. In M. Eastman (ed.), *Old Age Abuse*. London: Chapman & Hall.

George, L. (1986) Caregiver burden: conflict between norms of reciprocity and solidarity. In K. Pillemer and R. Wolf (eds), *Elder Abuse*. Dover: Auburn House.

George, L. (1989) Stress, social support and depression over the lifecourse. In K. Markides and C. Cooper (eds), *Aging Stress and Health*. New York: Wiley.

Gilbert, N. (1984) Welfare for profit: *Journal of Social Policy*, 13: 63–73.

Giles, H. and Coupland, N. (1991) *Language: Contexts and Consequences*. Buckingham: Open University Press.

Glendenning, F. (1993) What is elder abuse and neglect? In P. Decalmer and F. Glendenning (eds), *The Mistreatment of Elderly People*. London: Sage.

Goffman, E. (1961) *Asylums*. London: Allen Lane.

Goffman, E. (1963) *Stigma*. London: Allen Lane.

Goldner, V., Penn, P., Sheinberg, M and Walker, G. (1990) Love and violence: gender paradoxes in volatile attachments. *Family Process*, 29: 343–64.

Gouldner, A. (1960) The norm of reciprocity. *American Sociological Review*, 25(2): 161–78.

Grafstrom, M., Nordberg, A. and Wimblad, B. (1992) Abuse is in the eye of the beholder: reports by family members about abuse of demented persons in home care: A total population based study. *Scandinavian Journal of Social Medicine*, 21(4): 247–55.

Greenwell, S. (1989) *Whose Home Is It Anyway?* Bath: BUP.

Griffiths, A., Robert, G. and Williams, J. *et al.* (1993) Elder abuse and the law. In Decalmer, P. and Glendenning, F. (eds), *The Mistreatment of Elderly People*. London: Sage.

Griffiths, R. (1988) *Community Care: An Agenda for Action*. London: HMSO.

Gusfield, J. (1984) On the side: practical action and social constructivism in social problems theory. In J. Schneider and J. Kitsuse (eds), *Studies in the Sociology of Social Problems*. Norwood: Ablex.

Haber, C. and Gratton, B. (1994) *Old Age and the Search for Security*. Indiana: Indiana University Press.

Hadley, R. (1982) Origins of dissent. In T. Philpot (ed.), *A New Direction for Social Work*, London: Community Care.

Hall, P. (1987) Minority elder maltreatment. *Journal of Gerontological Social Work*, 9(4): 53–72.

Hallet, C. and Birchall, E. (1992) *Coordination and Child Protection*. London: HMSO.

Hamner, J. and Statham, D. (1988) *Women and Social Work*. London: Macmillan.

Hansard (1982) Written answer. *Hansard*, November.

Hargrave, T. and Anderson, W. (1992) *Finishing Well: Aging and Reparation in the Intergenerational Family*. New York: Brunner/Mazel.

Harris, I. (1981) *Americans Believe Government Should Take Major Responsibility in Coping with the Abuse Problem*, news release. New York: Harris Polls.

HMSO (1990) *The NHS and Community Care Act*. London: HMSO.

Hocking, D. (1988) Miscare – a form of abuse in the elderly. *Update*, 15 May: 2411–19.

Homans, G. (1961) *Social Behavior*. New York: Harcourt, Brace & Wold.

Homer, A. and Gilleard, C. (1990) Abuse of elderly people by their carers. *British Medical Journal*, 301: 1359–62.

Hooyman, N. (1983) Community interventions. In J. Kosberg (ed.), *Abuse and Maltreatment of the Elderly*. Boston: Wright.

Horn, P. (1976) *Labouring Life in the Victorian Countryside*. Gloucester: Allen Sutton.

Hornick, J., McDonald, L. and Robertson, G. (1992) Elder abuse in Canada and the US. In R. Peters (ed.), *Aggression and Violence Through the Lifespan*. Newbury Park: Sage.

Hudson, B. (1994) 'Training and abuse prevention'. Paper to the 2nd International Symposium on Elder Abuse, Stoke, September.

Hudson, M. (1986) Elder mistreatment: current research. In K. Pillemer and R. Wolf (eds), *Elder Abuse*. Dover: Auburn House.

Hudson, M. (1989) Analyses of the concepts of elder mistreatment. *Journal of Elder Abuse and Neglect*, 1(1): 5–25.

Hufton, O. (1967) *Bayeux in the Late Eighteenth Century: A Social Study*. Oxford: Clarendon Press.

Hufton, O. (1974) *The Poor in Eighteenth Century France, 1750–1789*. Oxford: Oxford University Press.

Hydle, I. (ed.) (1994) *Abuse and Neglect of the Elderly in their Homes – A Nordic Perspective*. The Council of Nordic Ministers Report, 94: 2.

Hydle, I. and Johns, S. (1992) *Closed Doors and Clenched Fists: When Elderly People are Abused in their Homes* (in Norwegian). Oslo: Kommuneforlaget.

Hytner, B. (1977) *Report into Allegations Concerning Moorfield Observation and Assessment Centre*. Salford: City of Salford.

Ignatieff, M. (1989) *A Just Measure of Pain*. Harmondsworth: Penguin.

Independent (1987) Pattern of death was sinister, report says. *Independent*, 22 July: 5.

Itzin, C. (1986) Ageism awareness training. In C. Phillipson, P. Strang and M. Bernard (eds), *Dependency and Interdependency in Old Age*. London: Gower.

Jack, R. (1992) Case management and social services. *Generations Review*, 2(1): 4–7.

Jack, R. (1994) Dependence, power and violation: gender issues in abuse of elderly people by formal carers. In M. Eastman (ed.), *Old Age Abuse*. London: Chapman & Hall.

James, A., Brooks, T. and Towell, D. (1992) *Committed to Quality*. London: HMSO.

Johns, S., Juklestad, O. and Hydle, I. (1992) 'Developing elder protective services in Norway'. Paper presented to the Ninth Annual Adult Protective Services Conference, San Antonio, Texas US.

Johns, S. and Juklestad, O. (1994) 'Research and action on elder abuse in Norway'. Paper presented to the 2nd International Symposium on Elder Abuse, Stoke, September.

Johnson, P., Conrad, C. and Thomson, D. (eds) (1989) *Workers versus Pensioners: Intergenerational Justice in an Ageing World*. Manchester: Manchester University Press.

Johnson, T. (1986) Critical issues in the definition of elder abuse. In K. Pillemer and R. Wolf (eds), *Elder Abuse*. Dover, MA: Auburn House.

Johnson, T. (1991) *Elder Mistreatment: Deciding Who is at Risk*. New York: Greenwood Press.

Jones, A. and Schechter, S. (1992) *When Love Goes Wrong*. New York: Harper Collins.

Jones, G. (1986) Training social workers to work with older people. In F. Glendenning (ed.), *Social Work with Older People*. Keele: Beth Johnson Foundation.

Kelman, H. (1973) Violence without moral restraint. *Journal of Social Issues*, 29: 30–41.

Kingston, P. (1994) 'Elder abuse: training implications'. Paper to the 2nd International Symposium on Elder Abuse, Stoke, September.

Kingston, P.A. and Penhale, B. (1994) Recognition of a major problem: assessment and management of elder abuse and neglect. *Professional Nurse*, 9(5): 343–7.

Kingston, P.A. and Penhale, B. (1995) *Family Violence and the Caring Professions*. Basingstoke: Macmillan.

Kivela, S.L., Paivi, K.S., Kesti, E., Pahkala, K. and Ijas, M.L. (1992) Abuse in old age – epidemiological data from Finland. *Journal of Elder Abuse and Neglect*, 4(3): 1–18.

Knight, B. (1986) *Psychotherapy with Older Adults*. Beverly Hills: Sage.

Kuhn, M. (1977) *Maggie Kuhn on Aging*. Philadelphia: Westminster.

Kurrle, S.E., Sadler, P.M. and Cameron, I.D. (1991) Elder abuse: an Australian case series. *Medical Journal of Australia*, 155: 150–3.

Kurrle, S.E., Sadler, P.M. and Cameron, I.D. (1992) Patterns of elder abuse. *Medical Journal of Australia*, 157: 673–6.

Kurz, D. (1993) Physical assaults by husbands. In R. Gelles and D. Loseke, *Current Controversies in Family Violence*. Newbury Park: Sage.

Lau, E. and Kosberg, J. (1979) Abuse of the elderly by informal care providers. *Aging*, 299: 10–15.

Laudrie, E. (1980) *Montaillou*. London: Penguin.

Law Commission (1993) *Mentally Incapacitated Adults and Decision Making: An Overview*. Consultation Paper 128, London: HMSO.

Lee, R. and Renzetti, C.M. (1990) The problems of researching sensitive topics. *American Behavioral Scientist*, 33(5): 510–28.

LeNavenec, C. (1994) 'Toward an integrative model of family managing styles'. Paper to SYSTED '94 Conference, Geneva.

Leonard, P. (1984) *Personality and Ideology*. London: Macmillan.

Leslie, A. and Fowell, I. (1988) A view of home help services. *Social Services Research*, 6: 18–26.

Llewellyn Smith, H. (ed.) (1934) *The New Survey of London Life and Labour Vol. VI*. London: P.S. King.

Lucas, E. (1991) *Elder Abuse and its Recognition amongst Health Service Professionals*. Hamden Court: Garland.

McCall, G. and Simmonds, J. (1966) *Identities and Interactions*. New York: Free Press.

McEwan, E. (ed.) (1989) *Age: The Unrecognized Discrimination*. London: Age Concern.

McEwen, K.E. (1994) Refining the intergenerational transmission hypothesis. *Journal of Interpersonal Violence*, 9(3): 350–65.

Maddox, G. (1977) Battered oldsters. *Arizona Daily Star*, 21 May.

Manthorpe, J. (1993) Elder abuse and key areas in social work. In P. Decalmer and F. Glendenning (eds), *The Mistreatment of Elderly People*. London: Sage.

Marx-Ferree, F. (1990) Beyond separate spheres. *Journal of Marriage and the Family*, 52: 866–84.

Means, R. (1992) 'User empowerment, older people and the U.K. reform of community care'. Paper to the Annual Conference of British Gerontological Society, University of East Anglia.

Means, R. and Smith, R. (1994) *Community Care: Policy and Practice*. London: Macmillan.

Medd, P. (1976) Committee of Inquiry into Incidents at Besford House. Shrewsbury: Shropshire County Council.

Milne, D., Pitt, I. and Neil, S. (1993) Evaluation of a carer support scheme for elderly people. *British Journal of Social Work*, 23(2): 159–68.

Minkler, M. and Robertson, A. (1991) The ideology of age/race wars. *Ageing and Society*, 11: 1–22.

Minkler, M. and Estes, C. (1992) *Critical Perspectives on Aging*. New York: Baywood.

Minois, G. (1989) *History of Old Age*. Cambridge: Polity Press.

Minuchin, S. (1974) *Families and Family Therapy*. London: Tavistock.

Mizra, K. (1991) Community care and the black community. In *One Small Step Toward Racial Justice*. London: CCETSW.

Monk, A. (1990) *Handbook of Gerontological Services*. New York: Columbia University Press.

Monk, A., Kaye, L. and Litwin, H. (1984) Resolving grievances in the nursing home. New York: Columbia University Press.

Montgomery, R. (1989) Investigating caregiver burden. In K. Markides and C. Cooper (eds), *Aging, Stress and Health*. New York: Wiley.

Moody, H. (1992) Bioethics and aging. In T. Cole, D. Van Tassel and R. Kastenbaum *Handbook of the Humanities and Aging*. New York: Springer.

Moody, H. (1993) What is critical gerontology and why is it important? In T. Cole, A. Achenbaum, P. Jakobi and R. Kastenbaum (eds), *Voices and Visions of Aging: Towards a Critical Gerontology*. New York: Springer.

Morley, R. (1994) Recent responses to domestic violence against women: a feminist critique. In R. Page and J. Baldock (eds), *Social Policy Review*, vol. 5. Kent: SPA.

Morley, R. and Mullander, A. (1992) Hype or hope? The importation of pro-arrest strategies. *International Journal of Law and the Family*, 6(2): 265–88.

Morris, J. (1992) Us and them? Feminist research, community care and disability. *Critical Social Policy*, 33: 22–39.

Moxley, D. (1989) *The Practice of Case Management*. Beverley Hills: Sage.

Mullen, C. and Von Zwanenberg, E. (1988) *Study of Television Viewing*. London: BBC Books.

Murphy, J. (1931) Dependency in old age. *Annals of the American Academy of Political and Social Science*, 154: 38–41.

National Health Service (1969) *Report into Allegations of Ill-treatment at Ely Hospital*. Cardiff – London: HMSO.

Nay, W. (1978) Intra-organisational roadblocks to behaviour modification programming. In D. Marholin (ed.), *Child Behaviour Therapy*. New York: Gardner.

Norman, A. (1983) *Rights and Risk*. London: Centre for Policy on Ageing.

Nussbaum, J. (1991) Communication, language and the institutionalised elderly. *Ageing and Society*, 11: 149–65.

Nussbaum, J., Thompson, T. and Robinson, J. (1989) *Communication and Ageing*. New York: Harper & Row.

O'Brien, J. (1985) 'The role of the physician in identifying and assisting abused and neglected elderly'. Symposium discussion; Meetings of the Gerontological Society of America, New Orleans, 23 November.

O'Hagan, A. (1993) Pee the Bed: Witchy-coo. *Independent*, 21 March: 20.

O'Leary, K. (1993) Through a psychological lens. In R. Gelles and D. Loseke (eds), *Current Controversies on Domestic Violence*. Newbury Park: Sage.

O'Malley, H., Segel. H. and Perez, R. (1979) *Elder Abuse in Massachusetts*. Boston: Legal Research & Services to the Elderly.

Obholtzer, A. and Zagier-Roberts, V. (1994) *The Unconscious at Work*. London: Routledge.

Ogg, J. and Bennett, G. (1992) Elder abuse in Britain. *British Medical Journal*, 305: 998–9.

Ogg, J. and Munn-Giddins, C. (1993) Researching elder abuse. *Ageing and Society*, 13(1): 389–415.

Pan, H., Neidig, P. and O'Leary, K. (1992) *Predicting Physical Aggression of Husbands Against Wives*. Stony Brook: State Universtiy of New York.

Parker, G. (1990) *A Typology of Caring*. York: SPRU, University of York.

Patel, N. (1990) *A 'Race' Against Time*. London: Runnimead.

Patel, N. (1994) Care or neglect in the care of the community? In R. Davidson and S. Hunter (eds), *Community Care in Practice*. London: Batsford.

Penhale, B. (1993) The abuse of elderly people. *British Journal of Social Work*, 23(2): 95–112.

Perring, C. (1991) 'Residential care and community care. Caring in homes initiative'. Working paper. Brunel University. Reading.

Phillips, L. (1983) Abuse and neglect of the frail elderly at home. *Journal of Advanced Nursing*, 8: 379–92.

Phillips, L. (1986) Theoretical explanations of elder abuse. In K. Pillemer and R. Wolf (eds), *Elder Abuse*. Dover: Auburn House.

Phillips, L. (1989) Issues involved in identifying and intervening in elder abuse. In R. Filinson and S.R. Ingman (eds), *Elder Abuse: Practice and Policy*. New York: Human Sciences Press.

Phillipson, C. (1982) *Capitalism and the Construction of Old Age*. London: Macmillan.

Phillipson, C. (1990) *Delivering Community Care Services for Older People*. Working Paper, 3. Keele: Keele University.

Phillipson, C. (1991) Intergenerational relations: conflict or consensus in the 21st century. *Policy and Politics*, 19: 27–36.

Phillipson, C. (1992) Family care in Great Britain. In J. Kosburg (ed.), *Family Care for the Elderly in a Changing World*. New York: Sage.

Phillipson, C. (1993) 'Elder abuse and neglect: social and policy issues'. Proceedings of the 1st International Symposium on Elder Abuse, Stoke.

Phillipson, C. (1994) Policy issues in elder abuse. Proceedings of the 2nd International Symposium on Elder Abuse, Stoke.

Phillipson, C., Bernard, M. and Strang, P. (1986) *Dependency and Interdependency in Old Age*. London: Croom Helm.

Phillipson, C. and Strang, P. (1986) *Training and Education for an Ageing Society*. Keele: Keele University.

Phillipson, C. and Biggs, S. (1992) *Understanding Elder Abuse: A Training Manual for the Helping Professions*. London: Longman.

Phillipson, C. and Biggs, S. (1995) Elder abuse. In P. Kingston and B. Penhale (eds), *Family Violence and the Caring Professions*. London: Macmillan.

Pillemer, K. (1986) Risk factors in elder abuse. In K. Pillemer and R. Wolf (eds), *Elder Abuse*. Dover: Auburn House.

Pillemer, K. (1993) The abused offspring are dependent. In R. Gelles and D. Loseke *Current Controversies on Family Violence*. Newbury Park: Sage.

Pillemer, K. and Wolf, R. (1986) *Elder Abuse: Conflict in the Family*. Dover, MA: Auburn House.

Pillemer, K. and Finkelhor, D. (1988) The prevalence of elder abuse: a random sample survey. *Gerontologist*, 28(1): 51–7.

Pillemer, K. and Moore, D. (1990) Highlights from a study of abuse of patients in nursing homes. *Journal of Elder Abuse and Neglect*, 2(1/2): 5–30.

Pillemer, K. and Hudson, B. (1993) A model abuse prevention program for nursing assistants. *Gerontologist*, 33(1): 128–31.

Podnieks, E. (1988) Elder abuse. In B. Schesinger (ed.), *Abuse of the Elderly*. Toronto: University of Toronto Press.

Podnieks, E. (1989) Elder abuse: a Canadian perspective. In R. Wolf and S. Bergman (eds), *Stress Conflict and Abuse of the Elderly*. Jerusalem: Brookdale.

Podnieks, E. (1992) National survey on abuse of the elderly in Canada. *Journal of Elder Abuse and Neglect*, 4 (1/2): 5–58.

Preston, S. (1984) Children and the elderly: divergent paths for America's dependents. *Demography*, 21: 435–57.

Pritchard, J. (1992) *The Abuse of Elderly People: A Handbook for Practitioners*. London: Jessica Kingsley.

Pritchard, J. (1993) Gang warfare. *Community Care*, 8 July: 22–3.

Quinn, M. and Tomita, S. (1986) *Elder Abuse and Neglect: Causes, Diagnosis and Intervention Strategies*. New York: Springer.

Rautman, A. (1962) Role reversal. *Geriatric Medical Hygiene*, 64: 116–20.

Richards, B. (1989) Visions of freedom. *Free Associations*, 16: 31–42.

Rights Not Charity (1992) Fascists attack disabled people, 1(2): 1–3.

Robb, B. (1967) *Sans Everything: A Case To Answer*. London: Nelson.

Roberts, S., Steele, J. and Moore, N. (1991) *Finding Out About Residential Care*. Working Paper. London: Policy Studies Institute.

Robertson, A. (1991) 'Nurse morale and quality of care of the demented elderly'. Proceedings of SYSTED 1991 Conference, Barcelona.

Robinson, B. (1983) Validation of a care giver strain index. *Journal of Gerontology*, 38(3): 344–8.

Rodwell, G., Davis, S. and Dennison, T. (1992) Images of old age on British television. *Generations Review*, 2(3): 6–8.

Royal College of Nursing (1992) *Whistleblow*. London, RCN.

Salter, B. (1994) The politics of community care. *Policy and Politics*, 22(2): 119–31.

Salvage, A., Vetter, N. and Jones, D. (1986) Attitudes to hospital care among a community sample aged 75 and over. *Age and Ageing*, 17: 270–4.

Salvage, A., Vetter, N. and Jones, D. (1989) Options concerning residential care. *Age and Ageing*, 18: 380–6.

Sanders, A.B. (1992) Care of the elderly in emergency departments: conclusions and recommendations. *Annals of Emergency Medicine*, 21(7): 79–83.

Savo, C. (1984) *Self-Care and Self-Help Programmes for Older Adults in the United States*. Health Education Council in Association with the University of Keele, Department of Adult and Continuing Education.

Schneewind, E. (1990) Reaction of the family to the institutionalisation of an elderly member. *Journal of Gerontological Social Work*, 15(1): 121–36.

Schön, D. (1987) *Educating the Reflective Practitioner*. New York: Jossey-Bass.

Scogin, F., Beall, C., Bynum, J., Stephens, G., Grote, N.P., Baumhover, L.A. and Bolland, J.M. (1989) Training for abusive caregivers: an unconventional approach to an intervention dilemma. *Journal of Elder Abuse and Neglect*, 1(4): 73–87.

Scruton, S. (1989) *Counselling Older People*. London: Edward Arnold.

Seccombe, W. (1991) *Milennium of the Family: Feudalism to Capitalism in Northwest Europe*. London: Verso.

Seebohm Report (1968) *Report of the Commission on Local Authority and Allied Personal Social Services*, Cmnd. 3703. London: HMSO.

Selzer, M. (1990) Role-reversal: you don't go home again. *Journal of Gerontological Social Work*, 15(1): 5–14.

Sheldon, J.H. (1948) *The Social Medicine of Old Age*. London: The Nuffield Foundation in association with Oxford University Press.

Sinclair, I. (1988) Elderly. In I. Sinclair (ed.), *Residential Care: The Research Reviewed*. London: NISW.

Sprey, J. and Matthews, S. (1989) The perils of drawing policy implications from research. In R. Filinson and S. Ingman (eds), *Elder Abuse: Practice and Policy*. New York: Human Sciences Press.

Stearns, P. (1986) Old age family conflict: the perspective of the past. In K. Pillemer and R. Wolf (eds), *Elder Abuse*. Dover: Auburn House.

Steinman, L. (1979) Reactivated conflicts with aging parents. In P. Regan, *Aging Parents*. Los Angeles, CA: USCP.

Steinmetz, S. (1988) *Duty Bound: Elder Abuse and Family Care*. Newbury Park: Sage.

Steinmetz, S. (1993) The abused elderly are dependent. In R. Gelles and D. Loseke *Current Controversies on Family Violence*. Newbury Park: Sage.

Steinmetz, S. and Amsden, D. (1983) Dependent elders, family stress and abuse. In T. Brubaker (ed.), *Family Relations In Later Life*. Beverley Hills: Sage.

Stets, J. (1990) Verbal and physical aggression in marriage. *Journal of Marriage and the Family*, 52: 501–14.

Stevens,A. (1994) *Communicating with Users. Back from the Wellhouse*. London: CCETSW.

Stevenson, J. (1977) *Social Conditions in Britain Between the Wars*. London: Penguin.

Stevenson, J. and Cook, C. (1977) *The Slump*. London: Jonathan Cape.

Stone, L. (1978) Walking over grandma. *New York Review of Books*, 12 May.

Straus, M. (1979) Measuring intra-familial conflict and violence: the conflict tactics scale. *Journal of Marriage and the Family*, 41: 75–88.

Straus, M. (1993) Physical assaults by wives: a major social problem. In R. Gelles and D. Loseke (eds), *Current Controversies on Family Violence*. Newbury Park: Sage.

Tatara, T. (1993) Finding the nature and scope of domestic elder abuse with the use of state aggregate data: summaries of key findings of a national survey of state PS and aging agencies. *Journal of Elder Abuse and Neglect*, 5(4):35–6.

Thobaben, M. (1989) State elder/adult abuse and protection. In R. Filinson and S.R. Ingman (eds), *Elder Abuse: Practice and Policy*. New York: Human Sciences Press.

Thomas, K. (1971) *Religion and the Decline of Magic*. London: Weidenfeld and Nicolson.

Thomas, K. (1976) Age and authority in early modern England. *Proceedings of the British Academy*, 62: 205–48.

Thompson, D. (1989) The welfare state and generational conflict. In P. Johnson (ed.), *Workers Vs Pensioners*. Manchester: Manchester University Press.

Thompson, F. (1945) *Lark Rise to Candleford*. Oxford: Oxford University Press.

Thompson, P., Itzin, C. and Abendstern, M. (1990) *I Don't Feel Old*. Oxford: Oxford University Press.

Thomson, D. (1984) The decline of social security: falling state support for the elderly since early Victorian times. *Ageing and Society* (4): 451–82.

Thomson, D. (1991) The welfare of the elderly in the past: a family or community responsibility. In M. Pelling and R. Smith (eds), *Life, Death and the Elderly: Historical Perspectives*. London: Routledge.

Tobin, S. (1989) The effects of institutionalisation. In K. Markides and C. Cooper (eds), *Aging, Stress and Health*. New York: Wiley.

Tomita, S. (1982) Detection and treatment of elder abuse and neglect. *Physical Therapy and Occupational Therapy in Geriatrics*, 2:2.

Tout, H. (1938) *The Standard of Living in Bristol*. Bristol: Bristol University.

Townsend, P. (1957) *The Family Life of Old People*. London: Penguin.

Townsend, P. (1962) *The Last Refuge*. London: Routledge & Kegan-Paul.

Townsend, P. (1981) The structured dependency of the elderly: the creation of social policy in the twentieth century. *Ageing and Society*, 1: 5–28.

Townsend, P. and Wedderburn, D. (1965) *The Aged in the Welfare State*. London: Bell.

Turner, B. (1993) *Citizenship and Social Theory*. London: Sage.

Twigg, J., Atkin, K. and Perring, C. (1990) *Carers and Services: A Review of Research*. London: HMSO.

United Kingdom Central Council for Nursing, Midwifery and Health Visiting (1994) *Professional Conduct – Occasional Report on Standards of Nursing in Nursing Homes*. London: UKCC.

US Administration on Aging (1993) *Survey*. Washington DC: US Administration on Aging.

US House of Representatives, Select Committee on Aging (1980) *Elder Abuse* (Report No. 96–261). Joint Hearing before the Senate Special Committee on Aging and House Select Committee on Aging, Second Session, 96th Congress, 11 June.

US House of Representatives, Select Committee on Aging (1981) *Elder Abuse: An Examination of a Hidden Problem* (Report No. 97–277). A report by the Select Committee on Aging, First Session, 97th Congress, 3 April.

Utech, M.R. and Garrett, R.R. (1992) Elder abuse and child abuse: conceptual and perceptual parallels. *Journal of Interpersonal Violence*, 7(3): 418–28.

Vinton, L. (1992) Services planned in abusive situations. *Journal of Elder Abuse and Neglect*, 4(3): 61–84.

Vousden, M. (1987) Nye Bevan would turn in his grave. *Nursing Times*, 83: 18–19.

Walker, A. (1980) The social creation of poverty and dependency in old age. *Journal of Social Policy*, 9: 45–75.

Wall, R. (1992) Relationships between the generations in British families past and present. In C. Marsh and A. Arber, *Families and Households: Divisions and Change*. London: Macmillan.

Wardhaugh, J. and Wilding, P. (1993) Towards an explanation of the corruption of care. *Critical Social Policy*, 37: 4–31.

Warnes, A.M. (1993) Being old, old people and the burden of burden. *Ageing and Society*, 13(3): 297–338.

Wenger, C. (1994) *Support Networks of Older People*. Bangor: Centre for Social Policy Research and Development.

Wertheimer, A. (1993) *Advocacy and Older People*. London: Centre for Policy on Ageing.

West, P., Illsley, R. and Kelman, K. (1984) Public preference for the care of dependency groups. *Social Science and Medicine*, 18(2): 287–95.

Wilkin, D. and Hughes, B. (1987) Residential care of older people: the consumer's views. *Ageing and Society*, 7: 175–201.

Willcocks, D. (1991) Criticism welcome. *Care Weekly*, 25 October: 10–11.

Willcocks, D., Peace, S. and Kellaher, L. (1987) *Private Lives in Public Places*. London: Tavistock.

Willmott, P. and Young, M. (1960) *Family and Class in a London Suburb*. London: Routledge.

Winner, M. (1992) *Quality Work with Older People*. London: CCETSW.

Wolf, R. (1986) Major findings from the three model projects on elderly abuse. In K. Pillemer and R. Wolf (eds), *Elder Abuse*. Dover: Auburn House.

Wolf, R.S. (1989) Testimony before the Subcommittee of Human Services: Select Committee on Aging. US House of Representatives Hearings on Elder Abuse.

Wolf, R. (1990) Testimony on behalf of the National Committee for the Prevention of Elder Abuse before the US House Select Committee on Aging. *Journal of Elder Abuse and Neglect*, 2(1): 137–50.

Wolf, R. (1992) Victimisation of the elderly. *Clinical Gerontology*, 2: 269–76.

Wolf, R.S. (1994) *Action on Elder Abuse*, Working paper no.1: A report on the proceedings of the 1st International Symposium on Elder Abuse. London: Age Concern.

Wolf, R.S. (1994) Responding to elder abuse in the USA. In *Action on Elder Abuse Working Paper No.1: A Report on the Proceedings of the 1st International Symposium on Elder Abuse*. London: Action on Elder Abuse.

Wolf, R. and Pillemer, K. (1989) *Helping Elderly Victims*. New York: Columbia University Press.

Wolf, R. and Pillemer, K. (1994) What's new in elder abuse programming? *Gerontologist*, 34(1): 126–9.

Woodhouse, D. and Pengelly, P. (1991) *Anxiety and the Dynamics of Collaboration*. Aberdeen: Aberdeen University Press.

Wright, M. (1993) *Training Programme for Elder Protection*. London: Tower Hamlets Social Services Department.

Wright, M. and Ogg, J. (1992) Challenging stereotypes. *Community Care*, 17 December: 21–22.

Yllo, K. (1993) Through a feminist lens: gender, power and violence. In R. Gelles and D. Loseke (eds), *Current Controversies on Family Violence*. Newbury Park: Sage.

Young, J. and George, J. (1991) A history of migration to the U.K. In A. Squires (ed.), *Multicultural Health Care and Rehabilitation of Older People*. London: Edward Arnold.

Index

AGE, RACE AND ETHNICITY
A COMPARATIVE APPROACH

Ken Blakemore and Margaret Boneham

This is the first definitive study of ageing among black and Asian people in Britain. Until now, debates on race relations have tended to ignore the 'greying' of Britain's minority communities. Equally, ageing studies have lacked a focus on the challenge realities of a multiracial society and of racial discrimination. In this wide-ranging and questioning book, the authors combine original research with the results of over a decade of community studies of age and race. They give a comprehensive overview of the British context of 'minority ageing', comparing it with that of other societies such as the USA and Australia. They show the range and variety of patterns of ageing in the Asian and Afro-Caribbean communities, illustrated by personal life histories, and there are substantial chapters on the challenges to be faced by the health and social services. This book will be essential reading, both for 'reflective practitioners' and for anyone concerned with new developments in the fields of ageing, race relations, sociology and social policy.

This is an important reference book for practitioners, professionals, gerontologists and students who want to gain an understanding of the realities, complexities and implications of providing comprehensive quality services for black and ethnic minority elders. . . The authors present significant social and demographic background studies from a range of sources. . . Professionals and students will find this book valuable as a research tool and for general information and further exploration of the subject.

I hope *Age, Race and Ethnicity: A Comparative Approach* finds its way into all good bookshops, social service libraries and every social policy and gerontology reading list. It is value for money.

(*Care Weekly*)

Contents
Introduction – Research, understanding and action – Comparative perspectives – Double jeopardy? – The Afro-Caribbeans' experience – The Asians' experiences – Health, illness and health services – Welfare and social services – Conclusion – Bibliography – Index.

176pp   0 335 19086 3 (Paperback)   0 335 19234 3 (Hardback)

AGEISM
Bill Bytheway

Ageism has appeared in the media increasingly over the last twenty years.

- What is it?
- How are we affected?
- How does it relate to services for older people?

This book builds bridges between the wider age-conscious culture within which people live their lives and the world of the caring professions. In the first part, the literature on age prejudice and ageism is reviewed and set in a historical context. A wide range of settings in which ageism is clearly apparent are considered and then, in the third part, the author identifies a series of issues that are basic in determining a theory of ageism. The book is written in a style intended to engage the reader's active involvement: how does ageism relate to the beliefs that the reader might have about older generations, the ageism process and personal fears of the future? To what extent is chronological age used in social control? The book discusses these issues not just in relation to discrimination against 'the elderly' but right across the life course.

The book:

- is referenced to readily available material such as newspapers and biographies
- includes case studies to ensure that it relates to familiar, everyday aspects of age
- includes illustrations – examples of ageism in advertising, etc.

Contents
Part 1: The origins of ageism – Introduction: too old at 58 – Ugly and useless: the history of age prejudice – Another form of bigotry: ageism gets on to the agenda – Part 2: Aspects of ageism – The government of old age: ageism and power – The imbecility of old age: the impact of language – Get your knickers off, granny: interpersonal relations – Is it essential?: ageism and organizations – Part 3: Rethinking ageism – Theories of age – No more 'elderly', no more old age – References – Index.

158pp   0 335 19175 4 (Paperback)   0 335 19176 2 (Hardback)

HEALTH IN OLD AGE
MYTH, MYSTERY AND MANAGEMENT

Moyra Sidell

- Why do many older people rate their health as good when 'objective' evidence suggests that old age is a time of inevitable decline and disease?
- How do different perspectives on health inform our understanding of health in old age?
- What are the policy implications for ensuring a healthy future for old age?

This book addresses important questions which existing literature on health and old age has largely ignored. By juxtaposing detailed case histories and first person accounts from older people with 'official statistics' on the health of 'the elderly' it explores the myths and tries to unpick the mysteries which surround the subject of health in later life. It goes on to explore the implications of these myths and mysteries for the way individual older people manage their health. It looks at the resources and social support available to them as well as the implications for public policy provision. The book ends by exploring the problems and possibilities of ensuring a healthy future for old age. It will be essential reading for reflective practitioners and for anyone concerned with the new developments in the fields of ageing, social policy and health.

Contents
Introduction – Part 1: The health context – The mirage of health – Lay logic – Patterns of health and illness among older people – Part 2: Experiencing health – Understanding chronic illness and disability – Maintaining health with physical illness and functional disability – Maintaining health with mental malaise – Part 3: Resources for health – Health care and the management of health – Personal resources and social support – A healthy future for old age – Bibliography – Index.

200pp   0 335 19136 3 (Paperback)   0 335 19336 6 (Hardback)